"Deciding what's best
for you and being
proactive allows you
to have more choices,
and therefore, make
better decisions."

"Be in control
of your future."

Steven F. Binder

# YOUR RECRUITING PLAYBOOK...

## Maximize Your Opportunities To Play College Sports

## Steven F. Binder

College Sports Recruiting Expert, Speaker
& Author For Over 30 Years

ISBN 978-0-692-88511-6

# DEDICATIONS

To my wonderful wife, Stacey, whose commitment, kindness and loving support I cherish every day.

To Stephanie and Carolyn, the joys of my life. Your motivation and successes have your mother and me in awe. I am so proud of you both. Keep the full-court press on.

# ACKNOWLEDGMENTS

I would like to thank the following people for their support along the way: Mom and Dad, and Nonnie and Pop-Pop, my loving and supporting parents and in-laws; Eddie, Kathy and Evan, for their valuable time and effort; and journalist Colby Brin, whose work has appeared on **espn.com** and **sportsgrid.com**, for his contributions. And all of the countless student athletes, parents, coaches, teachers, guidance counselors and school administrators who allowed me to help make a difference. Mentoring and working with young people is a passion of mine. Contributing to help guide their futures is a responsibility that I take very seriously, so, thank you, for allowing me to a part of your lives. Today's youth are tomorrow's leaders!

A.B. You are doing great…Keep following your dreams, you are a good one :)

# ABOUT THE AUTHOR

Steven Binder, nationally known expert, author and speaker on college sports recruiting has been helping student athletes, parents and coaches for over 30 years gain the necessary step by step knowledge for how to become a collegiate athlete. High school student athletes, parents and coaches need to take a proactive approach to recruiting because college coaches can't see all the potential players due to limited time and resources. As a result, many talented high school athletes do not get the opportunity to play college sports. This is why it is imperative to have a necessary action plan to recruit yourself.

Steven Binder speaks with college coaches and administrators nationwide and has found that they are all after the same thing: for parents and their student athletes to be realistic about the opportunity to play at the next level.

As a collegiate recruiting advocate, Steven has been helping and advising high school student athletes with the recruiting process for over 3 decades, placing thousands of student athletes at the college level. When it comes to the students, parents, and coaches who are involved in the collegiate athletic recruiting process, there's nothing Steve hasn't seen.

As a former college basketball academic all-american nominee from Curry College and the father of two collegiate athletes, Binder knows how complex the process can be for high school students and their families. Plus, with conducting recruiting seminars, providing individual guidance and running showcases, his advice is valuable to people taking action in this process. To help, Steven wrote *"Your Recruiting Playbook...Maximize Your Opportunities to Play College Sports"*. The Playbook is a step-by-step guide on how to get recruited for college sports. Steven is also featured on ESPN & WFAN as a college recruiting expert. To read more about Steven, his book & speaking events, please visit: www.stevenfbinder.com

## Contact Information
Email: **stevenbinder1@gmail.com**
Website: **stevenfbinder.com**
Twitter: **@stevenbinder1**
**Facebook.com/collegesportsrecruiting**

# TABLE OF CONTENTS

**Introduction**                                                     **15**
    What This Playbook Is About
    The X's and O's

**Chapter 1**   **Why You Should Recruit Yourself**          **18**
    "Blue Chip" Prospects vs. "Non-Blue Chip"
    Student Athletes

**Chapter 2**   **Who Is This Playbook For?**                 **21**
    Your Role in the Recruiting Process
    Choosing One Sport

**Chapter 3**   **The Key People**                            **24**
    The Student Athlete
    The Parents
    The High School/Travel Team Coaches
    The Guidance Counselors
    The College Coaches

**Chapter 4**   **The College Athletics Landscape**          **30**
    Know the Odds
    National Collegiate Athletic Association (NCAA)
    National Association of Intercollegiate Athletics (NAIA)

**Chapter 5**   **How to Use Social Media for Recruiting**    **35**
    The Do's and Dont's
    How To Effectively Use To Your Advantage
    What Are College Coaches Looking For

**Chapter 6**   **College Coaches Camps & Clinics**          **38**
                  **What Are the Advantages?**
    Is This a Recruiting Exposure Opportunity or Just
       a Regular Camp ? How To Tell The Difference
    What Should Be Your Expectations
    The Pluses and Minuses

**Chapter 7**   **Transferring: The Ins and Outs**           **41**
    The Positive and Negatives
    How Do I Decide What's Best For Me
    Action Steps To Consider

**Chapter 8**   **Recruiting Yourself: Pre-Game**            **45**
    Academic Growth
    Physical Growth
    Get Exposure
    The College Search and Selection

Familiarize Yourself with NCAA Rules and Guidelines
Assess your Academic Performance
Contacting College Coaches
Visiting Colleges and Meeting College Coaches

**Chapter 9      Recruiting Yourself: Game On      58**
Actively Recruiting Yourself to College Coaches
Communicating with College Coaches
Checklist: Responsibilities of Recruiting Yourself

**Chapter 10     Recruiting Yourself: The Home Stretch      65**
Finalizing Your List of Colleges
Gauging a Coach's Interest
Applying Early and Getting Offers

**Chapter 11     Recruiting Yourself: A Year-by-Year Timeline      70**
Freshman and Sophomore Years
Off-Seasons and Summers
Junior and Senior Years

**Chapter 12     Streamlining the Process as an Upperclassman      74**
Get the Ball Rolling
If You're a Senior Who's "Late to the Game"

**Chapter 13     Resource Center      76**
Official Websites So You Know the Rules and Guidelines
Planning Tools to Shape Your Future
Getting the Cost of College Funded

**Chapter 14     Recruiting and Video Services      78**

**Chapter 15     Rare Scenarios      80**
FifthYear Prep Schools
If You Get Hurt

**Chapter 16     Plays: Get Recruited      83**
Samples: Student Athlete Personal Profile
Sample: Introduction Email
Sample: During and End-of-Season Emails
College Coaches Contact List
Pros and Cons List
Important Actions Checklist

**Chapter 17     Some Final Thoughts      96**

**Chapter 18     Testimonials on Recruiting Yourself      98**

**Your Own Plays, Thoughts and Reminders      105**

# Stay in control of your future!

For additional & the latest recruiting information, tips, videos as well as contacting Steven to schedule a live speaking seminar at your school or event...please visit: **stevenfbinder.com** or email at **stevenbinder1@gmail.com**. Plus, schools, organizations & events can also receive discounts on books.

# INTRODUCTION

*There are so many kids who play high-school sports. There isn't much difference between many of them. So recruiting yourself goes a long way. It shows you're serious. The college coach thinks, "This is a kid I can work with. The other kid, I'm not sure—I'd have to make ten phone calls, five emails." Out of the 50 or so student athletes I've coached who have played in college, at least 30 of them were advised by Steven Binder.*
— Pat Mangan, Head Coach, Boys Basketball,
   Frederick Douglass Academy

## What This Playbook Is About

**H**ow will you stand out from thousands of other student athletes and get the attention of college coaches, so they want you on their teams?

How will you gain a major edge over thousands of other college applicants from high schools across the country?

The answer is what this playbook is all about: recruiting yourself to colleges based on your high school athletic career and your college potential—*whether or not you are already being actively recruited.*

Whether you know you want to be a college athlete, or you'd like to gain a major advantage in the college admissions process, recruiting yourself is the key. Recruiting yourself is the process where you are building relationships with college coaches during high school—where *you* are proactive about communicating with colleges, and where *you* own the process. Student athletes who actively communicate with college coaches are viewed favorably because they take the time to show their interest.

A recruited athlete has definite advantages over other non-athletes. Because it is necessary for elite athletes to spend a considerable amount of time working at their sport, college admission officers often modify the academic requirements generally necessary to get accepted. It could mean as much as a full letter grade or half a point to your grade point average, 3 to 5 points to your ACT score, or 300+ points to your total SAT score. Furthermore, you can receive a verbal offer of admittance to a college before non-athletes!

---

*Steven Binder has been a blessing to our program at Mount Vernon High School. At the Binderhoops Basketball Showcases, he is superb in his presentation to the student athletes. He lays out their priorities in a manner that is both easily understood and attainable. Steven is able to "cut through" all of the bad information out there and give each and every youngster a blueprint of what their course towards success should be. This is not only helpful to the "star athlete" but really beneficial to ALL of our players.*

*At our Mount Vernon Summer Camp, Mr. Binder has again given of himself to help our student athletes gain a better focus of the big picture. He does not ruin dreams, but he brings a focus on reality engaging our youngsters in a fashion to "attack their goals."*
*Steven has a gift for delivering his "pitch for success" with basketball, a little comic relief, and real life experiences all encompassed into one package.*
— Robert Cimmino, Athletic Director and Head Boy's Varsity
   Basketball Coach, Mount Vernon High School, NY

---

## The X's and O's

*Who is this playbook for?*

This playbook is for student athletes, but it also offers useful information for their parents, high school and travel team coaches, and guidance counselors. They all can play valuable roles in helping student athletes recruit themselves, and I'll tackle those roles in greater detail throughout the book.

*Do I have to start recruiting myself at a specific time?*

It's ideal to start the process in your freshman or sophomore year. The earlier you start, the more time you have to connect with college coaches and be seriously considered. If you are a junior or senior and you haven't started recruiting yourself yet, not to worry. While an earlier start is ideal, there are still many ways to make yourself an attractive candidate to both coaches and admissions counselors. Chapter 9: Streamlining the Process, discusses starting to recruit yourself in junior or senior year.

*Does it matter which sport I play?*

No. Colleges reserve spots on their sports teams for virtually every sport that student athletes play in high school.

*Does it matter if I'm being recruited already?*

This book will help the student athlete who is being recruited as much as the one who *isn't!* No student athlete is recruited by *every* school that would be a suitable match. This playbook can help you expand the pool of colleges that consider you—even if you're already being recruited.

*What about those recruiting services I hear so much about, that email coaches for you and let you upload video to their sites?*

Those services can be a help to some student athletes, but they are by no means absolutely essential. The services they provide do not eliminate the need to recruit yourself. While they can act as a nice supplement, nothing replaces the personal contact and relationship building that is required to set yourself apart from other athletes. The steps outlined in this book will help you build those relationships.

## Chapter 1
# WHY YOU SHOULD RECRUIT YOURSELF

*The more we hear from a recruit, the higher their chances are to make the team. It's like the saying "the squeaky wheel gets the oil." If a recruit is persistent with us, it shows they have a strong desire to be a part of our program and those are the types of kids you want. If you have a spot on the team and you are deciding who to give it to, it will probably be the visible, persistent recruit.*
— Corrie Falcon, Head Coach, Swimming and Diving,
    University of California, San Diego

*Recruiting yourself works. I had average talent and grades. By consistently communicating with college coaches, a trust was built, and I earned a spot.*
— Jennifer, basketball player, Rhode Island

Every college reserves spots for athletes. Every. Single. One. They all need to field athletic teams to increase their school's visibility, attract more students, provide diversity to student life, facilitate school spirit, and bring in additional revenue.

Every school offers traditional athletic scholarships or financial aid whether or not it is thought of as a "big time" sports school, is large or small, rural or urban, or is public or private.

College coaches are responsible for finding athletes to fill their rosters. However, many don't have the time or resources to recruit every single athlete they need. This is where *you* and the importance of marketing yourself enter the picture. With so many comparable athletes and with coaches having limited time and resources, it's important to show them who you are and why you are the best option for their school.

Believe me when I tell you that student athletes themselves can have a great impact in the college sports recruiting process. The student athletes who make themselves the *most visible* to college coaches will have the most influence. This playbook will show you how to be as visible as possible. Recruiting yourself will increase your chances of being selected by more colleges, so you'll have more choices when it comes time to make your final decision.

## "Blue Chip" Prospects vs. "Non-Blue-Chip" Student Athletes

Contrary to popular belief, you don't have to be a "blue-chip" athletic prospect, meaning one of the nation's best, to be admitted to colleges for sports. Most student athletes who fill college sports teams *are not* 24/7 athletics-obsessed jocks. Rather, they're simply students who excelled at one particular sport and want to continue at the collegiate level. The important thing to remember is that regardless of your athletic promise, all student athletes can benefit from recruiting themselves.

Top-rated athletes—even those who are actively being recruited by "big-time" colleges—can benefit from recruiting themselves. Even outstanding athletes cannot assume that they're being recruited to the best schools they can get into. Recruiting yourself might take a little extra work, but it can yield more choices of colleges that may have better academics or location or be a better fit athletically.

Then there are the students athletes we all read about in our local newspaper. These student athletes are the best in their high school and have an interest in playing in college but may not feel that they are good enough to be recruited. These students particularly benefit from reaching out and recruiting themselves because they may not have been seen or considered by college coaches. However, these student athletes often do have the ability and talent to make a college team.

Many student athletes receive recruitment letters and emails from prospective coaches. These letters are often sent out as mass mailings to hundreds of student athletes. Students often rely too heavily on these opportunities only to discover later that they were never honestly being considered—by which time their college options are more limited. It's equally important for these talented athletes to take an active role in their own recruiting process.

The bottom line: *All student athletes benefit from recruiting themselves— by making themselves consistently visible to college coaches.*

Chapter 2

# WHO IS THIS PLAYBOOK FOR?

---

*It's very important to get your name out there to the coaches. Email is a great way to communicate. In your sophomore and junior year, it's important to have contact with coaching staffs. We like to see enthusiastic student athletes. We love to coach student athletes who really want to be a part of our college and campus community.*

— Jeff Brown, Head Coach, Men's Basketball, Middlebury College

---

## Your Role in the Recruiting Process

Any student athlete with a passion to play a sport in college will attract the attention of college coaches if he or she follows my advice. But even student athletes who haven't yet considered playing in college will benefit. They should sit down with their parents and discuss the considerations I've outlined below. If the answer to many of the questions is a resounding "yes," then start recruiting yourself immediately. It is important to know yourself well enough to decide if this is something you should pursue.

- *Do you excel at your sport compared to other athletes of the same age in your city/state?*
- *Do you love playing your sport, and are you willing to make the commitment to get better?*
- *Will you commit to a training regimen and spend a significant amount of time on your sport beyond what you do for your high school team practices?*
- *Would you be willing to work year-round on body development and individual skills training?*
- *Would you play your chosen sport for a second team—such as travel, AAU or Elite leagues, or compete individually in*

*tournaments—in addition to your high school team?*
- *Would your family/guardian be supportive of your participation in a travel/club team?*

Beyond skill level and a desire to play in college, student athletes must be willing to devote the necessary time and effort into recruiting themselves. Skill, desire and commitment are equally important: Remove any one of those three, and the process won't work the best way it can.

It is very important for student athletes to know where they stand in relation to other athletes their age. Recruiting yourself only works within reason. Student athletes who do not excel locally will not be successful in recruiting themselves when they are competing against athletes from multiple cities and states for the same college spots, simply due to the available talent pool.

Club and travel teams, comprised of student athletes from neighboring towns, cities and states, compete in the off-season in tournaments against other teams from around the country. Participating in these large, regional or national tournaments are a great litmus test that will help gauge your ability amongst a broader group of athletes. Being a part of a club team is a commitment for both you and your family and it takes time and money. Club teams travel, generally by car, on weekends and during the summer to compete. Consider the costs and benefits of playing on these teams in your decision to compete at the next level.

## Choosing One Sport

Multi-sport student athletes should focus on recruiting themselves for one sport. I'm not suggesting you should stop competing in the other sports, but that you should only *fully* recruit yourself in one. (It is extremely rare for a student athlete to be recruited in two sports.)

After years of playing multiple sports, it might be difficult for some student athletes to choose one sport. To help yourself choose, decide which sport:

- You have the most individual success in
- You will work on the most on your own
- Better complements your academic school list
- You will intensely play and are willing to commit to throughout college
- You enjoy the most, because at the heart of this process is your enjoyment and satisfaction with your college experience.

## Chapter 3
# THE KEY PEOPLE

*Owning the recruiting process is the smartest thing you can do regardless of whether you are a Division I, II or III caliber athlete in any sport. Being proactive with college coaches about your interest, profile, ability and academics can help you with getting recruited. Also, staying engaged with the college team helps a student athlete show they are sincerely interested in that school. Coaches can tell when people have and have not done their preparation. Be your own best advocate, and stay informed.*
— Lindsay Gottlieb, Head Coach, Women's Basketball,
  University of California, Berkeley

**B**efore we get started on the actual process of recruiting yourself, let's go over the team of people you will work with in deciding which college is right for you. For the vast majority of student athletes your team will consist of parents or guardians, high school and travel coaches, guidance counselors and college coaches themselves.

## The Student Athlete

*I needed help. I did not know what to do. The internet has a lot of information, but it's not easy to understand. Recruiting yourself and proving yourself to college coaches allowed me to create opportunities. Thanks to Binder's process, my coach, my parents and I now understand what to do and how to take action.*
— John, football player, Texas

Ultimately, it's up to each student athlete to put in the necessary time, effort and dedication to recruit him or herself. The most engaged parents, high school coaches and guidance counselors can help, but they can't do the heavy lifting. That's up to only one person—the student athlete.

Here are the key responsibilities student athletes must take on to recruit themselves successfully:

- Maintain good grades to ensure that you will be eligible to be a recruited athlete. Be familiar with the NCAA guidelines regarding grades and other requirements (see *NCAA Guide for the College-Bound Student Athlete* in Chapter 4: The College Athletics Landscape).
- Show year-to-year improvement in grades. This will indicate effort and commitment to your academic performance.
- Achieve the best possible standardized test scores. Colleges have a wide range of test scores they will accept.
- Increase skill level in your chosen sport, which shows dedication and effort.
- Develop your body through physical and skills training.
- Consistently communicate and build strong relationships with key people:
  - Coaches
  - Trainers
  - Guidance Counselors
  - Mentors
  - Alumni
  - Anyone who could aid you in your journey.
- Research and visit schools to get a feel for your likes and dislikes.
- Maintain consistent, mature communication with coaches and other college officials.

## The Parents

*Steven Binder grounds the parents and players in critical thinking and planning. He stresses how recruiting yourself and building relationships with college coaches is key. His plan allows you to take immediate action.*
— Henry, parent of a high school athlete, Pennsylvania

*The recruiting process can be long and arduous; it's emotional and stressful. It's very important that the family band together and get started early with a plan.*
— Susan, parent of a high school student athlete, New York

Parents and guardians are vitally important to the recruiting process. Student athletes have to manage a lot, such as schoolwork, training, family commitments, and all of the other time obligations of high school life—which can often be overwhelming. These everyday stresses can prevent your child from putting in the proper time needed to maximize their recruiting options.

To help deflect some of that pressure, parents should:

- Always be encouraging and supportive, because the process can be disheartening.
- Help the student athlete stay calm and organized in all facets of his or her life.
- Help (if needed) with letter/email writing and other communications with colleges and coaches (cover letters, student athlete profiles, etc.). Remember that all communications *must* be in the "words and voice" of the student athlete.
- Schedule periodic meetings with your child and your child's guidance counselor to discuss college plans. Having a solid game plan often eases anxiety for both you and your child.
- Review the student's schedule and plan out college visits. Help make appointments to meet with coaches.
- Guide student athletes on interacting with college coaches; ask the child's guidance counselor to conduct practice interviews about meeting the coach.
- Be prepared with your own questions for college coaches, visit school websites and familiarize yourself and your child with the school.
- Be polite and courteous with college coaches and other officials.
- When in meetings with coaches, let your child lead the conversation, do not be overbearing, and contribute when needed.

## The High School/Travel Team Coaches

*So many good players and only a few spots ... we needed a smart way to get noticed by college coaches and scouts, and recruiting yourself was the difference maker for one of my players to be selected over someone else.*
— Manny, regional travel team coach, Illinois

High school and travel team coaches are crucial to the process in the same way that parents are; they can offer structure and a calming influence during a potentially stressful time. Here are some things high school and travel coaches may do to help:

- Help with training during the season and pre/post-season.
- Advocate on behalf of student athletes by calling or writing to college coaches, and give college coaches informative updates on student athletes as players.
- Act as an objective part of the process. Parents tend to be unconditionally enthusiastic and supportive advocates, no matter what's going on, and *they should be.* But having knowledgeable third parties who can give honest assessments, when necessary, also benefits the student athlete.

## The Guidance Counselors

Of course, guidance counselors are important to the college application process for everyone. But they can, and should, be helpful to student athletes because they serve as necessary liaisons between them and the admissions offices of colleges. They can also be an important ally to students, a supporter they can turn to for help in countless areas: managing their school work load, ensuring they are taking the proper classes, preparing for and scheduling standardized tests and working on interview skills. They are also a resource to answer questions such as: what schools should I look at? What should I ask a coach? What should I wear to a school visit? How can I find out about scholarships/financial aid?

Guidance counselors should have reliable contacts in college admissions offices. Student athletes will be communicating primarily with coaches, who might sometimes be evasive. Ultimately, guidance counselors should be able to speak directly to admissions officers to find out whether or not a spot is truly being reserved for a student athlete. I'll explore this further later on.

## The College Coaches

College coaches themselves are the ultimate gatekeepers. It is they who will go to the admissions officers at their respective colleges and recommend the student athletes for admission. However, keep in mind:

- College coaches do not have enough time to see and evaluate all of the high school athletes that could be great assets for their schools.
- Due to NCAA rules, coaches may only contact student athletes on a very limited basis (see "contact period" on page 32). *However, these rules periodically change.*

---

### Time-out

Student athletes *are* permitted to contact coaches as much as they'd like. That's the whole point of recruiting yourself: *Increasing your visibility with as many college coaches as possible will improve your chances of being selected for their programs.*

---

## What College Coaches Look for in a Potential Recruit

To understand why it works to recruit yourself, it's important to know what sports recruiting is like for the college coaches. College coaches need skilled players to fill their teams' roster. Beyond that, they want fundamentally sound athletes who are versatile and can play more than one position in their given sports.

*Can the baseball catcher also play first base if need be? Can the sprinter also perform in the triple jump? Can the volleyball middle blocker also play the setter?*

College coaches value this adaptability because it allows for flexibility within their existing roster. This is important in case of player injury or ineligibility due to poor academic performance. Being versatile could help you to be an even more attractive recruit, and could separate you from the recruits you're competing against. That being said, excelling at one particular position or skill is also a valuable asset.

Most importantly, coaches are looking for student athletes with skills and character who show the potential to improve and are coachable. Having a strong work ethic is key because coaches want players who, four years down the line, will be even better than they are today.

## What College Coaches Don't Like
- Unresponsiveness
- Cockiness
- Lack of passion
- Indifference—be clear on *why* you want to go to this *specific college.*
- Dishonesty about grades—there is no getting around eligibility. Your transcript is the only official document a college will review with regard to grades. Don't waste a coach's time by overstating your grades.
- Poor work ethic.

Coaches have seen it *all* before. Don't even try to fool them on *anything*!

Chapter 4

# THE COLLEGE ATHLETICS LANDSCAPE

*When I first started thirteen years ago, a lot of recruiting was done by going to see a student athlete play, by word of mouth, or referrals. Now the majority of the initial contact is through recruiting services or through student athletes themselves.*
— Matt Magers, Head Coach, Baseball, Minnesota State

L et's take a short look at the world of college athletics so you can get a sense of where you logically fit.

## Know the Odds

- Roughly 3 to 5 percent of high school athletes will play a sport in college. The specific number is almost impossible to pin down, and odds vary greatly across the different sports.
- Many talented players will not play in college *because they do not recruit themselves* by contacting college coaches on their own.

Contact from college coaches can take many different forms. The following table is a rough guide that illustrates the type of communications and their frequency. It makes it clear that being recruited to play college sports is challenging.

| Communication Type | Number of Prospects* |
|---|---|
| Receive a questionnaire from a particular college | 2,500 + |
| Receive follow-up contact/emails | 350 out of 1,000+ |
| Receive a phone call from a coach | 75 out of 1,000+ |
| Are on the repeat call list | 35 out of 1,000+ |
| Are asked to visit campus | 25 out of 1,000+ |
| Receive official support from admissions office | 3+ out of 1,000+ |
| Are admitted to the college | 3 out of 1,000+ |

*Varies by sport

Despite the odds against any individual prospect getting into college through athletics, they get astronomically higher *if you do nothing. However, they improve if you're proactive in communicating with college coaches directly.*

## National Collegiate Athletic Association

The National Collegiate Athletic Association (NCAA) is the governing body that oversees sports and athletic championships at approximately 1,200 colleges and universities in the United States and Canada. It's important for student athletes and their families to review the NCAA website and read the *NCAA Guide for the College-Bound Athlete*, which can be downloaded for free: **ncaapublications.com**. High school athletes who want to play college sports at a Division I or II must register with the NCAA. The NCAA website is a great resource for information. All student athletes and their families should familiarize themselves with the rules and logistics associated with their sport.

Below are some key terms you need to know regarding the recruiting process. This information comes from the *NCAA Guide*.

> ***NCAA Division I, II and III:*** The NCAA is made up of three membership classifications that are known as Divisions I, II and III. Each division creates its own rules governing personnel, amateurism, recruiting, eligibility, benefits, financial aid, and playing and practice seasons. Every program must affiliate its core program with one of the three divisions. One of the differences among the three divisions is that colleges and universities in Divisions I and II *may* offer athletic scholarships, while Division III colleges and universities do not. An exception to this rule would be the colleges in the Ivy League. The eight schools in this Division I program do not offer athletic scholarships but can offer aid base on merit or need. However, an important point to keep in mind is playing collegiate athletics at any level will have a year-round commitment.

**Please note: Scholarships can be offered in both full and partial amounts and are *renewed annually*.** If you are fortunate to receive an athletic scholarship, make sure you are clear about what you are getting.

The NCAA membership includes approximately 340 Division I schools, 290 Division II schools, and 440 Division III schools.

***Recruiting coordinator/assistant coach:*** Every college sports team has a coach who serves as the point person for recruiting.

***Contact period:*** During this time, a college coach may have in-person contact with you and/or your parents on or off the college's campus. The coach may also watch you play or visit your high school. You and your parents may visit a college campus and the coach may write and telephone you during this period.

***Evaluation period:*** A college coach may watch you play or visit your high school, but cannot have any in-person conversations with you or your parents off the college's campus. You and your parents can visit a college campus during this period. A coach may write and telephone you or your parents during this time.

***Quiet period:*** A college coach may not have any in-person contact with you or your parents off the college's campus. The coach may not watch you play or visit your high school during this period. You and your parents may visit a college campus during this time. A coach may write or telephone you or your parents during this time.

***Dead period:*** A college coach may not have any in-person contact with you or your parents on or off campus at any time during a dead period. The coach may write and telephone you or your parents during this time.

***Official visit:*** Any visit to a college campus by a college-bound student athlete or his or her parents paid for by the college is an official visit. During an official visit the college can pay for transportation to and from the college for the prospect, lodging and three meals per day for both the prospect and the parent or guardian, as well as reasonable entertainment expenses including three tickets to a home sports event. This is generally done during the senior year in high school.

*Unofficial visit:* Visits paid for by college-bound student athletes or their parents are unofficial visits. The only expenses a college-bound student athlete may receive from a college during an unofficial visit are three tickets to a home sports event. These visits can take place at any time during high school. In fact, they are encouraged so the student athlete can see what they like and do not like at each college. The earlier you visit colleges, the more time you will have to evaluate your potential options.

*Verbal commitment:* This phrase is used to describe a college-bound student athlete's commitment to a school before he or she signs (or is able to sign) a National Letter of Intent. A college-bound student athlete can announce a verbal commitment at any time. While verbal commitments have become very popular for both college-bound student athletes and coaches, this "commitment" is NOT binding on either the college-bound student athlete or the college or university. Only the signing of the National Letter of Intent accompanied by a financial aid agreement is binding on both parties.

*National Letter of Intent:* The National Letter of Intent (NLI) is a voluntary program administered by the NCAA Eligibility Center. By signing NLI, the college-bound student athlete agrees to attend the college or university for one academic year. In exchange, that college or university must provide athletics financial aid for one academic year, renewable each year.

## National Association of Intercollegiate Athletics (NAIA)

Similar to the NCAA, the NAIA is a governing body of colleges that compete in intercollegiate athletics throughout the United States and Canada. The NAIA has nearly 300 member schools and more than 60,000 student-athletes. NAIA schools are generally smaller and are often located in the Midwest. Their admission requirements are less rigorous than those found at NCAA schools. It is divided into 25 conferences and offers 23 championships in 13 sports. NAIA schools offer both athletic scholarships and academic scholarships. Student athletes interested in playing for a NAIA school need to register with NAIA Eligibility Center. Please review the following websites for more information on NAIA:

Link to the *NAIA Guide for the College-Bound Student Athlete:* **naia.org**

Link to the NAIA Eligibility Center: **playnaia.org**

Chapter 5

# HOW TO USE SOCIAL MEDIA FOR RECRUITING

## The Do's and Don'ts

Social media is becoming the "email" norm of recruiting. College coaches are now placing their emphasis and efforts towards social media platforms because of its usability and immediate response time. As a result, recruits must think about the proper ways in which to use social media to their advantage, rather than have it serve as their downfall.

Social media has become a game-changing factor when it comes to recruiting, as it can help you as a player to gain further exposure. Having viable and interesting content to share with coaches can be a major advantage for you. With that being said, it is important to remember, whether posting athletic or social content, there is "no getting it back." Be active but be careful, truthful, and show integrity.

It is also important to be aware not only what you put on your social media accounts, but to also pay attention to what college coaches choose to publicize as well. Everyone from fans, boosters, and players from a school you are considering may attempt to influence your collegiate decision through heavily promoting the different aspects of their schools through social media. Therefore, it is important to not be overly influenced by what you see. Remember, this is your recruitment process. The more you stick to the basics and not worry about outside influences, the better for all parties involved.

## How to Effectively Use to Your Advantage

Here are six key principals for how best to use social media to your advantage:

1) **Use social media to promote yourself as a well-rounded individual:** If you have extra curricular activities outside of the sport you play, showcase those as well.

**2) Use it to your benefit:** Look to these platforms as another means to gain exposure. For example, post about: a big win that just took place, a video clip displaying athletic skills, or a rivalry game coming up. You can also mention something of significance that happened with a college team that you have interest in. Making the conversation as much about them, as you, is a good way to increase dialogue.

**3) Beware of high school social media policies**: Some high school athletic departments have social media guidelines. Check to see if yours does and what they restrict from a team perspective. For individual postings, just be mindful of the school and team you represent.

**4) Don't be like everyone else:** Show your ability to be a free and critical thinker. Just because the world is re-tweeting or posting something that may be funny or interesting, doesn't mean you have to.

**5) Use platforms to ask coaches questions:** It won't take long to see if they are interested in you or what you have to say.

**6) Avoid conflict with fans:** Fans are called that for a reason, it's short for fanatic. Don't engage in conversations with fans that you don't know. Stay positive or do not say anything at all.

With that being said, everything posted online, whether good or bad, has the potential to damage a recruit's chances at scoring a scholarship, receiving financial aid, or even being admitted to a school all together. Assume that someone at a school's compliance office or a college coach is monitoring what you say or post on social media.

## What College Coaches Are Looking For

While expressing one's beliefs is certainly within their rights, coaches don't necessarily want to be put in a position where they are having to defend someone who isn't even on their roster. For instance, be careful when posting content regarding controversial topics such as religion or race relations, as what you say may be interpreted negatively by others.

**Always remember:**

- Deleting something means nothing. Someone is only a screenshot away from ruining a recruit's dream of obtaining a scholarship.

- If more than one school is recruiting you, be cautious not to publicly post photos of yourself on athletic visits (whether official or unofficial) to other schools. Do not feel the need to "share" everything. Play it quiet sometimes.

- Parents, before your child decides to post anything, look it over. Think to yourself and discuss with your child, "would I want this published on the front page of the New York Times?" If the answers is no, then don't post it.

- If you re-tweet or share it, you better own up to it. You can put all the warnings you want to online, such as "RTs do not equal endorsements," but in college recruiting, perception is reality, and coaches don't have time to ask parents or the student athlete what their stance is concerning what they post on social media.

- Be cognizant of the NCAA's social media rules. See **http://www.ncaa.org/student-athletes/future/recruiting** for more information.

- For the parents who also have social media accounts: be cautious about what you post about your child. Don't over promote-coaches do not like when parents are overbearing. It could be the downfall of your child's recruiting process.

Where social media can be a powerful medium for communication, I have seen it ruin students' collegiate athletic careers. Just be smart—if you are unsure, then do not post at all. Social media can have more detrimental consequences than benefits if not handled properly.

Chapter 6

# COLLEGE COACHES' CAMPS & CLINICS: WHAT ARE THE ADVANTAGES?

## Is This a Recruiting Exposure Opportunity or Just a Regular Camp ? How to Tell the Difference

Before deciding whether or not to attend college coaches' camps or clinics, it is important to understand the reason in which you are attending and what you hope to get out of it. Is it to improve your skills? Attend with your teammates? Or, to gain exposure with the hopes of being recruited by that particular school? Being able to set your expectations is crucial because attending these events cost time and money. Once you come to that resolution, talk to the coach and see if you are on the same page.

With that being said, it is important to do your research. What and who is the camp for? Some camps, for instance, just focus on improvement of skills and technique while other camps are used primarily for recruiting and comparing talent. Thus, know what you are signing up for. Keep in mind that just because you attend these camps does not mean you will realistically be seen. In other words, there may be many other players attending—so being recruited for that particular school may be more difficult. To avoid wasting your time and money, talk to the coach beforehand to ask about your position or situation in their recruiting process. Open and candid conversations are not only acceptable, but necessary. Yet, be prepared for answers you may not want to hear—it is better to find out sooner than later so you can move on to other potential schools.

If after the conversation with the coach, you choose to attend the camp, ensure you make the most out of your time there, on and off the court. Don't be afraid to go up to the coaches and current players on their roster and introduce yourself, be engaging. Coaches will often ask their current players (who are typically present at the camps) about their thoughts on potential recruits. Coaches are not only recruiting you as an athlete, but also as a person.

## What Should Be Your Expectations

Here are some questions you should be asking coaches in regards to the college coaches' camps before you make the decision for whether or not to attend:
1) Why do you need me to attend?
2) How interested are you in me as a player?
3) Am I priority recruit for you?
4) What will it take for you to offer me a spot on your team?
5) Will college coaches from other schools be in attendance?
6) (After the camp ask:) When would be best for me to follow up with you regarding how I performed at the camp and potential next steps?

If you attend the camp, and after the coach communicates his or her increased interest, be sure to continue that open dialogue. Do not be afraid to ask questions about next steps regarding where you fall in their recruiting process. For instance, Does he or she have spots left in your recruiting class? If so, be sure to directly ask about potential playing time as a freshman, if that is a priority for you. Whatever the answer a coach gives, it is important to remember that your development and the other players the coach is bringing in could also impact your playing time. With that said, it is good to ask these questions early so there are no major surprises if you choose to attend that school.

## The Pluses and Minuses

Recruits in many sports, male and female, are now making their commitments earlier in their high school careers, whether it is through a verbal or an early signing period. This could affect other recruits' standings, which is why it is crucial to ask the questions mentioned above.

Be candid in a respectful and kind way because no one wants to waste his or her time, energy and money. Don't be afraid to ask the tough questions—you deserve that honest feedback from coaches!

**Chapter 7**

# TRANSFERRING: THE INS AND OUTS

## The Positives and Negatives

Transferring, whether it be to the same or lower division school, could greatly benefit someone who has taken the proper steps to ensure their success at this new school. Here, just like in the original recruiting process, it is absolutely crucial to do your homework. Be able to honestly answer some key questions such as: What are you transferring away from? What does this new school have, athletically and academically, that your current school does not? Weigh your pros and cons so you do not end up transferring and find yourself in the same situation that you were in at your previous school. Although there are many reasons for why student athletes choose to transfer, a considerable amount do so because they did not have the proper information on how to effectively navigate the recruiting process in high school. Therefore, when transferring, ensure you take the necessary steps to avoid making the same mistake again.

## How Do I Decide What's Best for Me?

Here are some significant data points that reflects the frequency of transferring within the NCAA:

- According to the NCAA, 40% of all college basketball players who enter Division I directly out of high school depart from their initial school by the end of their sophomore year.
- For the 2015-16 season, 528 Division I basketball players transferred, according to ESPN.
- Only 44% of those players transferred to another Division I school. The remainder transferred to Division 2 or 3 Schools, or to the NAIA (National Association of Intercollegiate Athletics).

It is important to research not only the school and athletic program, but also the NCAA rules. When transferring between divisions, a student athlete may have to sit out a year. Here are the transferring guidelines for schools in the NCAA:

You must sit out a year if you transfer from:
- Division 3 to Division 1 or 2
- Division 2 to Division 1
- Division 1 to Division 1
- Division 2 to Division 2

You do not have to sit out a year if you transfer from:
- Division 1 to Division 2
- Division 1 to Division 3
- Division 2 to Division 3
- Division 3 to Division 3

Generally speaking, college student athletes have four years of athletic eligibility and have 5 years to complete it (although there are medical exceptions at times). Make sure to visit the NCAA website for latest rules on transferring.

## Action Steps to Consider

If you are thinking about transferring, one of the first things you should do is check with your current school on restrictions for leaving. Some schools won't allow inter-conference transfers, and others may not release a player from a scholarship, for whatever reason. Note: Division 3 schools do not require releases, you can proceed without direct permission. Check with your current school, and the school you are potentially transferring to, to understand the regulations and logistics. But keep in mind the consequences of asking your current coach for you to be released for your team; they may not have you back if you do not end up transferring.

You will need to be granted your "transfer release" BEFORE you begin officially talking to other coaches. This is important because you do not want to put your eligibility status at risk. Most players indeed receive their release from their current school, but sometimes schools deny it. So, handle your departure process and requests with dignity and respect, which is sometime difficult to do during an emotional time. But, please remember- they have what you want, which is your release to go to another school. As you know, it's easier to attract more bees with honey.

With that said, it is important to weighs the pros and cons and do your homework. Keep in mind, that freshman year of college, especially for an athlete, is hard. Sometimes, transferring is not the solution, patience is. Coaches can leave or get fired, giving you another opportunity with a new coach without having to transfer. If transferring is want you ultimately decide, do as much research as possible beforehand to ensure happiness and success at this new school so that the same mistake is not made twice. Do things like talk extensively to the coach, research the academics of the school, look online at the roster, and even consider reaching out to student athletes that have transferred. They will be able to provide valuable insight about how they felt and what they would have done differently in their selection process. Learning from others can be invaluable.

Another option is to be a graduate transfer. This allows student athletes to complete a bachelor's degree before exhausting their athletic eligibility status. In other words, you can graduate from a university in three years and still have that one year of athletic eligibility remaining. Therefore, you can go on to pursue a graduate degree on a potential athletic scholarship or financial aid. Although not common, it is another viable option to keep in mind and plan for if that is an academic goal of yours.

Here are some things to consider when transferring (which are similar in principle to when you were being recruited as a high school athlete):
- Have an understanding of where you can fit into the playing rotation by candidly speaking with the coach and looking at

the team roster. Have you spoken to the coach about playing time? Are there seniors graduating at your position? How many freshmen is the coach planning on bringing in the following year? These are all indicators of what your potential role would be on this new team.

- Is the academic environment right for me? Do they have offer areas I want to study? Viable internships available for student athletes?

Further, now that you are older and already well into your collegiate experience, it is important to be able to answer these three key questions as well:

- What are my main goals for attending a different school?
- Would I be happy here if I did not play a sport? (Refer to the chapter in the book, "The Broken Leg Test" for additional information on this topic).
- Do the coaches also support the players off the athletic field? For instance, are players able to get internships to gain valuable work experience during the summers? Do they have an established and engaged alumni network?

Even if you don't play a single minute, getting a quality education should be at the top of the priority list. College is a forty-year decision, not just a four-year decision. Therefore, it is crucial to keep in mind all that is mentioned in this chapter when you are considering whether or not to transfer.

## Chapter 8

# RECRUITING YOURSELF: PRE-GAME

*Every year, we start with 15,000 to 20,000 student athletes nationwide who fit our profile for football. On any given day, I get between 10 and 15 emails from prospects. If they're from my area, I try to watch their video immediately, and look at their profile. The more information and contact with the coaches, the better. You can never get too much information out there about yourself. All things being equal—academics, skill-set, position—if we know a recruit is extremely interested in Dartmouth, then that would definitely increase his stock.*

— Christopher Wilkerson, Head Coach Football Coach, University of Chicago (formerly Recruiting Coordinator, Dartmouth College)

**T**his chapter details the initial steps you should take to begin the process of recruiting yourself. Ideally, student athletes should start the process of recruiting themselves during their freshman or sophomore year. But that is simply the ideal scenario. Student athletes should work the process as much as possible whenever they decide to start recruiting themselves. They can begin the process during the junior year and even the beginning of senior year. The window of time in which they can make a difference will simply be smaller. If you start communicating with college coaches in your freshman or sophomore year, you will have a longer time to get to know each other and you'll have a greater opportunity to make an impression on them. Likewise, you will have a longer time to develop your body and your skills in your chosen sport.

First, there are two things every student athlete should be working at throughout high school: academic and physical growth.

## Academic Growth

Make sure you're taking all the core courses necessary to play college athletics. Guidance counselors are key here since they are familiar with the various college requirements.

Not all student athletes are A students, but it's important for you to either show consistent improvement from year to year in high school or continue to maintain your good grades. So don't get discouraged if your grades are less than stellar at first. College admissions officers like to see students who learn from their mistakes and develop themselves academically as they move through high school. College coaches like student athletes who prove their character in the same way.

Additionally, it is important to write down your academic goals. This is to evaluate where you are now academically and confirm whether or not you meet the academic standards to be eligible.

## Physical Growth

This is as important as academic growth. By playing on high school and club teams and competing in tournaments, student athletes will naturally develop their skills in their chosen sports. It's equally important to develop your strength and conditioning as well as your individual skills. College coaches want well-rounded, athletic players. As you did with your academic goals, compile a list of your athletic goals. Evaluate your strengths and weaknesses and put together an action plan to ensure continued development. A good person to help you with this would be your high school coach or club coach.

These days, conditioning—speed, strength, agility, quickness and endurance—is more important than ever. College coaches want versatile, highly athletic players on their teams. That's why you need to engage in a physical conditioning program that will ensure that by the time you're a senior in high school, your body will match up with fellow prospects.

*Now let's go over the actionable steps of recruiting yourself.*

## Get Exposure

**Play on a Travel or Club Team or Compete Individually
in Tournaments**
Here are a few examples:

- Basketball: Showcases/Tournaments (**aauboysbasketball.org,
  aaugirlsbasketball.org**)
- Golf: USGA Junior Tournaments (**ajga.org**, AJGA College
  Recruiting Guide)
- Tennis: USTA Junior Tournaments (**ustaserves.com**)
- Lacrosse: Invitational/Team Camps (**uslacrosse.org**)
- Football: Combines/Team Camps (**usafootball.com**)
- Softball: Travel/Elite Teams (**asasoftball.org**)
- Fencing: **usfencing.org**

All sports have showcases or tournaments for college exposure.
Check with your club, regional or national sport organizations for
recommendations.

If you are not sure which is right for you, here are some ideas to try and
find the best experience possible: Speak with your high school coach
and reach out to members in your community to help compare one
program to another. You can also discuss options with a college coach.
You want to try and find the best program possible for college exposure.

It's crucial for student athletes to know where they stand, not just in
their particular high school leagues, but also in secondary leagues—
such as club teams and travel teams—which include student athletes
from neighboring towns and cities and states. Student athletes can't
know how good they are at a particular sport from playing only on their
high schools teams, they have to compete on a more regional or
national level. Find out which teams attract the most competitive
players and try to get on those teams.

**Play in Showcases/Tournaments**
Recruiting yourself is all about making yourself more visible to college

coaches. Showcases are independently run venues that allow you to play your sport in front of college coaches and against other players in your sport. They offer you the unique opportunity to get exposure to many coaches at one time and evaluate your ability against other athletes. You'll want to attend individual showcases/tournaments that:

- Are attended by a significant number of college coaches. Find this out by asking people who have attended these showcases themselves and by asking high school and college coaches which ones they like.
- Have a good ratio of scouts to players. Playing time is very important. How much time will you spend on the court or field, as opposed to standing on the sidelines? Note: Smaller showcases can be better for this reason—it's easier to get noticed—as long as college coaches will actually be there!

Again, do a little background research via the internet and word of mouth (talk to high school and college coaches, for starters) on any tournament/showcase you're thinking of attending. Once you decide which individual or team showcase to attend, email college coaches and let them know where you are playing; this is a great opportunity to increase your visibility.

Note on "elite" college camps: Carefully consider which, if any, college camps you attend. Frequently, coaches send out mass mailings and invite student athletes to attend. This invitation to attend is often misinterpreted by student athletes or their parents as being recruited. Attend these camps if you are very interested in a particular school or have had dialogue with that school's coach about being a recruit. Elite camps can be expensive; you do not want to waste valuable time and money if you are not confident that a college coach is very interested in you or if you don't meet the academic requirements of a particular college. Ask them, because it's better to know the truth before you register. However, quite often, coaches from other colleges and universities who are in non-competing divisions may attend these elite camps so it maybe an opportunity to get additional exposure. For example, Division II and III coaches may attend a Division I elite camp to scout talent and look for players. So if you know that a certain coach will be attending a particular camp, it may be worth your time and expense.

## The College Search and Selection

Student athletes should explore and consider the usual factors in choosing the colleges to which they apply. Students should not pick their list of schools simply for their athletic programs. No student athlete should attend a college that they wouldn't otherwise like to attend, if sports weren't involved. There are no right answers here; choosing schools is based on personal fit.

Here are some things to consider when putting together your list of schools:

- Big schools vs. small schools
- Urban schools vs. rural schools
- Close to home vs. further from home
- Offers the curriculum your interested in studying
- General feel of campus, students, professors and academics
- Opportunities beyond sports to grow as a person
- Alumni networking (internships, career counseling, etc.). (Alumni, especially sports alumni, truly "bleed school colors" and are almost always enthusiastic about helping student athletes during the school year and after they graduate.)
- Rapport with coaching staff and team.

---

### Time-out

When putting your college list together you may need to consider whether or not financial aid or athletic scholarships are a factor. Most Division I and II colleges, as well as NAIA schools, can offer athletic scholarships and all schools offer financial aid based on need or academic merit.

---

If you are considering Division I or Division II colleges you must register with the NCAA Eligibility Center. This is done to help ensure your academic and amateur status. Begin this process in the beginning of your sophomore year. You will continue to update your eligibility status throughout high school, with the last requirement being to submit your final transcript. You can register online at **eligibilitycenter.org**. (Likewise, if you are interested in a NAIA school, you will need to register with their eligibility center at **playnaia.org**.)

### The Broken Leg Test

If you have any doubt about whether or not a particular college is right for you, apply the "broken leg test": Would you be happy to attend this college even if you had a broken leg and couldn't play any sports there? This is important, because:

- You might not see as much playing time as you'd like.
- Coaches can leave for different schools or get fired (hopefully not!).
- You might actually get injured (hopefully not!).
- You're young and your interests are changing. What seems like an ideal athletic situation now might not always be that way.
- Going to college is about your personal growth, not only any one sport.

---

**Time-out**

Make sure to reach out to current or former players/students and alumni, to see what a particular college is like from their "insider perspective."

---

### Athletic Considerations

Even though every student athlete should attend a school that passes the broken leg test, there are still athletic considerations to take into account:

- Does the college team need the position you play?
- Who else are they recruiting for your position?
- Do you like and feel comfortable with the coaching staff?
- How important is playing time to you?

## Assess Your Athletic Ability

It is important to be aware that there are many talented players from around the country vying for the coveted recruiting spots on college teams. When making your list of colleges, it is crucial to honestly and fairly assess your ability. What you don't want to do is overstate or overemphasize your personal talent level. If you do, you will have less of a chance of being recruited and your playing time could be reduced.

---

### Time-out

Speak with your high school/club coaches, college coaches that are on your list, and scouting services to help gauge the appropriate level. For example, if feedback states that you are a low Division I player, it would be wise to include Division II and Division III schools on your list. You may have the talent to make a team's roster, but not the talent to receive quality playing time. This is a personal decision; there is no right answer. Simply put, just decide what you want your athletic experience to be in college.

---

## Team Rosters Don't Lie

Visit the team's official website to answer the two questions below:
- How many seniors are graduating?
  - Look at the current roster. This will tell you how many spots are opening up for your class.
- How many underclassmen athletes play your same position?
  - This will give you an idea of how many student athletes you will be competing against for your specific position.
  - This is also where your ability to play more than one position becomes particularly valuable as a prospect.

Weigh these two numbers (seniors graduating and teammates playing same position) to assess how much the coach needs someone at your position. For instance, if you're a left-handed pitcher, and most of the team's left-handed pitchers are graduating, that coach needs someone like you. On the other hand, if most of the team's left-handed pitchers are freshmen and sophomores, you might be the best left-handed pitcher in your class, but the coach won't have as much of a need for you simply based on your position. This speaks to why it pays to be a versatile athlete who can play more than one position, and why it pays to do proper research.

I'm not saying that you should give up on schools that don't have openings at your position—only that you should weigh that factor with others.

If you are very interested in playing for a specific coach but it appears that team doesn't need a recruit at your position, it doesn't hurt to ask: "Coach, what kind of player are you looking for?" This should lead to a more in-depth conversation that might answer some questions that the roster alone cannot answer. In general, developing a dialogue with a coach can help you build a solid relationship—which is invaluable in recruiting yourself to that college.

## Familiarize Yourself with NCAA Rules and Guidelines

The NCAA is the governing body that was founded to protect student athletes from being treated unfairly. NCAA policies govern how coaches can recruit college-bound student athletes to ensure a fair playing field. The rules specify when and how coaches can contact prospects, what materials can be sent and when student athletes can visit campus. The rules differ from sport to sport. (See **ncaa.org**.) Knowing your sport's NCAA specifics and rules is critical for recruiting success. Do your homework using the NCAA website. I can't emphasize this enough. Prospective student athletes must meet minimum academic standards and amateurism criteria to play college sports. Better to know early what grades and standardized test scores you need to be eligible and what actions could affect your amateur status.

## Assess your Academic Performance

It is important to be honest with where your grades are as early on as possible. If you got off to a slow start, it can take several semesters of better grades to bring up your GPA. If your grades and your SATs/ACTs do not meet NCAA eligibility minimum requirements, you will not be able to be recruited by Division I, II or III schools immediately out of high school.

An option here can be to attend a community or junior college. Be aware, if you decide to play your sport at the community/junior college level, it will reduce your four years of eligibility by the amount of years that you play. For example, play one year at the community/junior college level and you'll have three years of eligibility remaining at a four-year school. This can also be a great option for financial reasons, to stay close to home or if you feel you're not ready athletically or academically for a four-year college. If these situations pertain to you, then use the same *Your Recruiting Playbook* action steps to apply to a two-year college. (See the National Junior College Athletic Association (**njcaa.org**) website for more information.)

## Contacting College Coaches

Once you've made a list of colleges in which you have an interest, you can start contacting college coaches.

Every college sports team has a recruiting coordinator. This is usually an assistant coach on the team, but in some cases, it may well be the head coach. To find the recruiting coordinator, first call the school's athletics office, and someone there will refer you to the right person. Or you can review the team's homepage on the school's athletics website, which might identify the recruiting coordinator.

The recruiting coordinator will provide the student athlete with the necessary contact information for the head coach of the given sport (unless the head coach is the recruiting coordinator) and any other information pertinent to communicating with that coach, and the athletics office.

Your first contact with any coach should be via email. See Chapter 16: Plays, for a sample introductory email.

If it's unclear who the recruiting coordinator is, or which coach is the appropriate one to contact, you can write your introductory email to the entire staff. Just make sure that the name of the head coach is in the "To" line of the email and the assistant coaches should be in the "CC" line.

**Time-out**

1. You should review the biographies of all the coaches on the teams that interest you. You never know what you might have in common with one of them. One of the coaches may have graduated from your high school, or maybe another shares one of your hobbies. That would be a good person to contact, even if he's not the head coach or recruiting coordinator. You want as many coaches as possible in your corner!

2. Due to NCAA rules, which vary by sport, coaches might not be able to call you back until your junior year. However, recently the NCAA made a policy change, which now allows for texting. This should help communication flow a bit more freely. But in any case you shouldn't feel like you're being ignored when a message of any kind goes unreturned. College coaches are extremely busy! Remember: Even when coaches aren't allowed to reach out to you—or may not have the time—you're always allowed to reach out to them whenever you'd like. As you'll see, doing so is one of the most important parts of recruiting yourself!

## Visiting Colleges and Meeting College Coaches

By the end of his or her sophomore year, the student athlete should have a list of 10 "reach" schools, 10 "target" schools, and 10 "safety" schools. This list can and will change over time. Your guidance counselor and coach can help identify these three categories of schools. Start constructing this list as early as possible and start communicating with college coaches and visiting campuses as soon as possible.

Even with all of the great reference guides and research materials available, there is no substitute for meeting coaches and seeing campuses first hand. Communicating with a coach and visiting a campus shows your interest in a school. An important part of recruiting yourself is illustrating that genuine interest. Coaches want student athletes who are enthusiastic about playing for them.

---

### Time-out

Fill out *all* questionnaires you receive from college coaches, whether online or through the mail, even if you are not interested in the school or have never heard of it. Because your list is always changing, your interests and goals may change and college coaches also change, especially assistants. College coaches change jobs all the time. Building a base of contacts will help you stay ahead of the game. Again, knowledge is power.

---

When you visit a campus, try to meet with a coach—or at least with someone on staff if the head coach is unavailable. You don't want to miss the opportunity to put yourself on the coach's radar. Call ahead and see if someone from the coaching staff would be available before finalizing your campus visit. These meetings typically last 30 minutes to one hour.

Student athletes must always keep in mind that college coaches will evaluate their personality and character as much as their athletic skill. These meetings, though informal, might be as important as any on-field performance. So when meeting with a coach, make sure you do the following:

- Are prompt and courteous. Show up on time—actually, make sure you arrive early.
- Bring a pad and pen to take notes, which shows how much you care about what the coach has to say.
- Dress casually but appropriately, and always neatly. It's better to be overdressed than underdressed.
- Shake hands firmly and look the coach in the eye.
- Have at least three questions to ask a coach during the introductory meeting, to show your engagement and sense of

responsibility. (Plus, you need information!) Here are three basic questions you can ask:

– What are you looking for in a student athlete?

– What's your recruiting timeline for selecting players?

– I want to play for you. What are the next steps I should take?

Make sure you bring the following materials to your introductory meeting:

- The latest copy of your profile (see example of a student athlete profile in Chapter 16: Plays)
- A copy of your transcript (you can get this from your guidance counselor)
- Game DVDs—full- and half-games.

Give these materials to the coach in a folder with your name on it. Of course, these items can be sent electronically, but for many coaches, nothing replaces a tangible record that they can hold in their hands.

At the end of the meeting, you should be appreciative and thankful for the coach's time, shake hands, and ask for a business card. Within 24 hours, send the coach a thank-you note (can be via email or regular mail). Most prospects don't do this. It's a show of character, and yet another way to distinguish yourself.

---

**Time-out**

Remember that in all interactions with college coaches, it is very important for the student athlete to show that he or she is a responsible young person in how he or she acts and communicates. This is another quality that can help the student athlete stand out from other recruits. Not all recruits will come off as mature young adults. Make sure *you* do!

---

### Questions the College Coach Might Ask

Of course, the college coach will also want to ask you questions. Again—and this can't be stressed enough—college coaches are looking for strong character, interest in their college, and intellect as much as for athletic skill. You must be ready to answer the following questions clearly and confidently—and truthfully. College coaches want to see an accurate representation of you.

- What are you looking for in a college? (Do some homework: review college websites/talk to fellow students.)
- What kind of student are you? What are your grades like? (Bring a current copy of your transcript.)
- Describe your strengths and weaknesses as a player.
- What other colleges are you looking at?
- Who will be involved in your decision?
- What defines a good teammate or leader?
- Do you have some DVD's that I can look at?
- What questions do you have for me about this college?
- What do you want to study?
- Why are you a good fit for this college?
- Why would you like to attend this college?

## Questions Parents Should Ask

Generally, student athletes and their parents will meet coaches together. Parents should ask at least a few questions, to further cement the student athlete's interest in the school. Here are some suggestions for the parents' questions:

- What do you expect from your players?
- How is academic and athletic balance achieved? What, if any, academic support is there for athletes—mandatory study halls, etc.?
- What is the four-year graduation rate?
- What do your players do for fun? How do they develop other interests?
- How can alumni help with internships?
- How do you prefer to interact with parents and players during the season and off-season?

# Chapter 9
# RECRUITING YOURSELF: GAME ON

*We want contact from the athletes! We want the athlete to be proactive, to take the initiative. If they can't pick up the phone to call or it's too much to return an email, I don't know that they're going to have that work ethic that we desire out of a student athlete. You can never bug a college coach too much. Unless they told you that they don't have a spot for you in their program. The more initiative you take, the more you show your desire to be in their program, the better. I'm looking for something that sets an athlete apart.*
—Jennifer Mills, Head Coach, Women's Volleyball, Clarion University

When you have a good sense of which colleges most interest you and the coaches for whom you'd most like to play, you can begin to actively recruit yourself. Keep in mind:

- College coaches collect as many names and contacts as possible, from as many sources as possible, including high school coaches, camps, AAU and online questionnaires. You will also receive reams of material from colleges while you are recruiting yourself.
  - Fill out *any* materials you receive from *any* college, even if you have no interest in going to it. You never know where that college's coach might end up in the future, and you don't know which coaches communicate with each other. Plus, your own interests could change. Keep all your options open.
- From your very first contact, you are being evaluated athletically, academically and personally. College coaches could also request game videos, transcripts, test scores and game statistics, so have all of these updated and ready at all times.
- The NCAA has strict guidelines that cover written communication, email, texts, phone contact and campus visits, as well as official and unofficial home visits. These rules often change, so stay informed.

- Generally, college coaches might not be able to contact you until your sophomore or junior year. Besides, they're always very busy, which means most communication with them will be one-way, although the new rule change, allowing for texting, should mitigate this a little. Again, it's all about making yourself visible.
- The college athletics recruiting process isn't always fair. Take two student athletes, with identical credentials. Both might get into a school, or one might, or perhaps neither will. This unfairness also can work to your advantage—*be mindful of your interaction with coaches, admissions officers, players and peers. Stand out as a mature, promising young student athlete!*
- College coaches will watch your behavior and actions on and off the court. How you behave and communicate is as important as your talent.
  - For example: *Are you supportive of teammates? Respectful of opposing players? Do you help players get up when they're knocked down? Do you show frustration if you're not playing well or do you keep your composure?* As one college coach told me: "You can't teach character."

Now that we've covered those basic but important conditions, let's talk about how you can get noticed as that respectful, coachable, versatile, talented, skilled athlete that coaches want to play for them.

## Actively Recruiting Yourself to College Coaches

*There are so many good players out there. I needed to stand out. Recruiting yourself works and helps build relationships with college coaches.*
—Sarah, soccer and lacrosse player, California

While college coaches are generally restricted to call student athletes, the exception is during limited periods when the student athlete is an upperclassman. But since student athletes are always allowed to call and email coaches, go for it. For one thing, opening up a line of communication to a coach will get you into the coach's mind—it will literally get them to begin *thinking of you.*

It's therefore important to establish as many touch points as possible with coaches, for example:

- Emails
- Postcards
- Visits
- Letters
- Phone calls
- Handwritten notes

Additionally, feedback from coaches will help you improve your appeal as a prospect. It will help you discover what you need to do, what's really important to the particular coaches you speak to, and what you might *not* need to do.

## Communicating with College Coaches

You should consistently email and call any college coach for whom you want to play. Emailing coaches frequently, especially during the high school and travel-team seasons, is not only okay—it is encouraged. Coaches want to hear from student athletes.

How frequently? You should make contact at least ten times a year or more (per school) by sending the following:

- An introductory note
- An early-season note
- Several in-season notes
- An end-of-season note
- A note with final grades
- Updates on events, results, awards, travel team season and community service activities, etc.

These emails or handwritten notes can cover many subjects, including:

- How school is going for you
- A big upcoming game
- Your team's schedule
- Awards
- Current events (shows you have other interests)
- A big win
- An academic achievement

- An athletic achievement
- Being selected as captain of your team (shows leadership)
- Game DVD
- Your community service
- How your team is doing
- High school schedule
- Camps/clinics you're attending
- A desire to come to campus. ("I'm looking to come to campus in a few weeks, will you be around?" or "I might be at the School A versus School B game, will you be there?" After a visit, send the coach an email, even if you didn't see him.)

I've heard many coaches say they like it when students write to them about their college programs. Here are some suggested topics you can write about:
- When an assistant coach is hired
- A big upcoming game
- A noteworthy event regarding that college (find news about the school on the internet)
- The college coach or the program reaches a milestone
- A big win
- A rivalry game

**The Grandparents Test**
When it comes to athletic and academic achievements, don't email college coaches or other college officials news that only means something to your grandparents. Your grandparents might be interested that you studied hard all week, or that you're looking forward to next week's game against your school's rival, but these general tidbits won't inspire a college coach.

Instead, think of writing something like: "Dear Coach – I had a very interesting homework assignment this week that made me think of why I'd love to play for your team so much." In other words, make your communications relevant to them.

**Time-out**

1. When emailing college coaches, always include all of your contact info: email, phone number, and mailing address. Make it as easy as possible for these coaches to contact you.
2. The communication you have with certain members of a school's coaching staff may differ from one to another; every staff is different. But no student athlete gets recruited to a school if the head coach is not on board. If you're not comfortable with how your communication with a particular head coach is going, be cautious recruiting yourself to that school.

Use your best judgment when communicating with coaches and staffs. Stay inside the lines, but if you get to know a particular coach, and you think you have zeroed in on a great way of communicating with him or her, go for it!

### Letters

If you really want to distinguish yourself from fellow prospects, sending a college coach a hand-written letter, instead of one or two emails, will go a long way. There is no substitute for something coaches can hold in their hands.

### Game DVDs

Send the entire game, not just highlights. Let the college coaches decide how much they want to watch. Include your contact information and a photo of yourself on the DVD cover.

**Time-out**

If taking video is something you don't feel capable of doing properly, you don't necessarily have to use a video service. You can usually find another student or local hobbyist to take film for you, inevitably at a much lower cost than the professional services. Your school may also tape your high school games and may be able to provide you with a copy.

### Additional Meetings with Coaches

Generally, if a student athlete meets with a coach, and receives significant interest, a second meeting should take place. This is a great opportunity to follow up with a coach.

A student athlete who actively schedules visits with college coaches is usually received enthusiastically since coaches appreciate interest. But you should only visit a college coach more than once if he or she shows interest in *you*.

In subsequent meetings with a coach, you might want to ask questions including:

- Have your player needs changed?
- Am I a priority recruit?
- What is the off-season commitment for your team?
- How many other players are you recruiting at my position?
- Can you or alumni help with internships?
- What are the most important qualities you look for in players?
- What academic/financial support do you give student athletes?
- If I commit to you, will you commit to me? (This can be a bold but effective move. It can be done after several emails, conversations and other feedback. If you don't get the answer you want, ask what the next steps would be, or move on to another college coach.)

### Academic and Athletic Growth

This cannot be stressed enough: it is *crucial* for the student athlete to keep exhibiting the ability to improve and progress as a student, athlete and person, all through the process of recruiting yourself.

### Checklist: Responsibilities of Recruiting Yourself

Make sure you're doing the following:

- Stay in contact with the coaches and colleges you really like. Send out letters of introduction, your profile, game DVD's, club schedule, high school schedule, transcript, press clippings and letters of recommendation.

- Update your profile throughout the year, as new information comes up. Updates provide yet another opportunity to email college coaches and *build relationships*—that's a good thing!
- Call or email coaches on packets you sent to solicit feedback. Inform them when and where your club/travel team is playing in tournaments.
- Have your high school coach, club/travel coach or school advisor call and email colleges on your behalf. Your high school and travel coaches can talk about your character, work ethic, particular skills, and your strengths and weaknesses as a player. Communicating to a college coach your skill level—especially the areas in which you need to improve—will give a lot of credibility to the conversation. This way the coach has a clear picture of who you are and what you can bring to the team.
- Fill out all online questionnaires and respond to all information. *You never know!*
- Make unofficial visits through your sophomore and junior years and official visits when you're a senior. *This helps differentiate what you like and shows coaches you have real interest.*

**Chapter 10**

# RECRUITING YOURSELF: THE HOME STRETCH

*I much prefer getting an email or phone call directly from a prospect or his coach as opposed to from a recruiting service that just sends blanket emails to every school in the country. I want to know, A: That they are interested in our institution, and, B: Why they are interested in our institution. I want them to let me know in that first brief introductory email that they have researched our institution and that they know something about it and that they know it is a possible fit academically, socially, and geographically, etc.*
—Trevor Andrews, Recruiting Coordinator and
   Defensive Line Coach, Football, College of William and Mary

## Finalizing Your List of Colleges

**B**y the middle of your junior year—and at the latest, the fall of your senior year—you will have visited colleges, been in communication with coaches and programs, and hammered out a final list of desired schools. Now is the time to start gauging the actual interest of those colleges, so you can know where you should—and should not—focus your efforts.

Of course, all along, during the previous years, you have probably been getting feedback from college coaches in the natural course of communicating with them. Using your best judgment, you'll probably be able to tell where you stand with each coach. But if you can't tell exactly where you stand, there are a few ways to find out.

## Gauging a Coach's Interest
*Interpreting Communications*

| Contact from Coaches | Level of Interest |
|---|---|
| Mailed personal contact (could be a mass mailing) | Almost none |
| Request for tape/transcript/H.S. or club schedule | Some |
| Phone contact, hand-written note | Stronger |
| Unofficial/official visit at coach's request | Very strong |

## Find Out Where You Stand

After you've been in contact with a coach for a full season—or, let's say, four or five emails—that coach should have some feeling for you as a student and athlete. Beginning in your junior year, you should start asking the coach where you stand with that college. I recommend that you do this with a phone call or in person, rather than email, because coaches will be more frank with you if you talk with them live versus through email.

Here are some suggestions for questions you might ask during that conversation:

- Am I a key prospect on your list?
- Where do I rank?
- If I was making my final list, do you want your college to be included?
- If I commit to your school will you offer me a scholarship? (Or admission to the school through the admissions office?)
- Do you see me in the playing rotation as an underclassman?

---

### Time-out

When you talk to a college coach, listen well. Try to read between the lines. *What is being said? What's not being said?* (For example, is the coach bringing up your potential playing time—or not? Is the coach expressing clear interest in you—or not?) If, in the end, you are still unsure of where you stand after speaking with them, ask: "What would you like me to take away from this conversation?" or "Coach, do you want me on your team?"

---

Remember always to be respectful and kind when communicating with a college coach. At the same time, keep in mind that direct and truthful dialogue is important. Neither of you wants your time wasted! If you ask in a straightforward manner, most coaches will tell you where you stand. Generally speaking, if they waffle, they're noncommittal to you. If they are consistently unresponsive to messages, hedge their answers, or are otherwise "unhelpful," they're noncommittal. If you walk away from that conversation still unsure where you stand in their eyes, they're non-committal. Use your best judgment to decide if a college seems out of your reach.

If this is the response you are receiving, here are a few ideas to try:

- Contact the college coach and ask them why they are no longer interested. Stress to them that you want honest feedback so you can learn.
- Ask college coaches if they could recommend you to another school. All college coaches have contacts and relationships. They can be a terrific resource for you. If you were trying to be a Division I prospect, they could suggest other Division II and III schools that may be a better fit.
- Reach out to scouting services that may have rated you, because they know you as a player and they know coaches and their needs.
- Meet with your guidance counselor; you may have over-reached with your list of schools. You may need to adjust your 10–10–10-school list then reach out to your new list of schools via email and send out game films.

**What *Not* to Do**

Don't play the "I have other offers" card with college coaches—whether you do or you don't. No one, including any college coach, wants to be put in a corner like that. The end result of such "threats" will likely be the coach dropping you from their list for being difficult and/or arrogant. Don't make anything resembling a threat or ultimatum to any coach at any time! (This goes for parents, too, of course.)

> **Time-out**
>
> You *can* mention that other colleges or conferences have strong interest in you. This is even recommended—as long as you do it in a polite, respectful way.

### Guidance Counselors

Your guidance counselor can also play a valuable role here. While student athletes will be communicating primarily with coaches, who might sometimes be evasive, guidance counselors should be able to speak directly to admissions officers, to find out whether a spot is truly being reserved for a student athlete or not, or to attain general information on a college's admissions requirements for recruits. College admissions officers and high school guidance counselors have an important relationship. This could be very helpful to you!

### Applying Early and Getting Offers

*Once I became a recruited athlete, the process allowed me more choices and I went to a better college than I thought was possible.*
—Brendan, baseball player, Florida

Applying early to a college can sometimes dramatically increase your odds of admission if you're certain you want to attend that school. If you like a college enough, and are willing to commit to it, I recommend telling the coach just that: "Coach – if I commit to you, will you support my application for admission?" *(This should be done during the junior or senior year.)*

In the fall of your senior year, you will join your classmates in applying to colleges, or colleges might offer you a spot. That could have come as early as your junior year. By now, you will hopefully have an offer from a coach, or multiple offers, and you are aware of the pros and cons of each school.

Again, before submitting an application to a college you assume you will be admitted to based on sports, you need to make sure the admissions office is on board. Your high school guidance counselor and the college coach are key here. *You want to close the loop, to leave no doubt.*

After you close that loop, that college's application will be, in effect, paperwork. Now it's up to you!

## Chapter 11

# RECRUITING YOURSELF: A YEAR-BY-YEAR TIMELINE

*If we're looking at two players with the same ability, and we can't take them both, obviously the one who shows more interest, who comes to visit first, is going to be higher on our list. Being proactive is absolutely going to help. Every level is different... When I was at a smaller division one school, we would go watch most student athletes who wrote to us, especially the ones who played in a specific position that was needed at that time.*
—Tatum Clowney, Assistant Coach, Women's Soccer,
   University of Alabama

This chapter lays out the preferred timeline for recruiting yourself by maximizing the opportunities available to you.

### Freshman and Sophomore Years

Here are some objectives for your freshman and sophomore years:
- Write down your academic goals.
- Grow academically each year.
- Write down your athletic goals.
- Get exposure by playing in tournaments or on a travel or club team.
- Sign up to play in showcases. Recruiting yourself is all about making yourself more visible to college coaches.
- Start developing physically and continue to develop all four years.
- Go to NCAA.org and familiarize yourself with the rules.
- Start thinking about which colleges you'd like to attend. Meet with your guidance counselor, make them aware of your interest to play collegiate sports, and start forming a list of schools.

- Make first contact with the recruiting coordinators or assistant coaches at the desired colleges:
  - Introduce yourself and provide your contact information.
  - Ask what's important to them and their needs in your recruiting class.
  - Possibly meet with them on campus visits.
  - Send them game DVDs—full games or halves (not highlights, which make it seem like you're cherry-picking which plays to show).
- Visit schools (when possible) to see what is out there.
- Learn about the different standardized tests: SAT, SAT Subject Tests and ACT. The criteria differ from one school to another. There are many colleges and universities that are test optional.
- By sophomore year, sign up to take a practice PSAT(SAT) or PLAN(ACT) test. Your guidance counselor can help you with this.

## Off-Seasons and Summers

The summers and the off-seasons between sports are good times to work on things that are difficult to focus on when school is in full swing. In the off-seasons, you should aim to:
- Gain feedback from coaches on your abilities and progress
- Work on developing your body/skills
- Play on a travel or club team
- Take on an internship, job or volunteer job
- Visit colleges, to see some campuses and meet coaches
- Continue to prepare for standardize tests
- Review and edit your list of schools.

## Junior and Senior Years

Junior year is crucial in the process of recruiting yourself—both academically and athletically. This is the year when the rubber really begins to meet the road, and the bulk of the work of recruiting yourself takes place. Recruiting yourself is like taking on the workload of another academic class. During this year you should do the following:

- Email and call college coaches regularly. *Evaluate your conversations with these coaches to get a feel for where you stand with each; learn to decipher exactly what the coach is telling you.*
- Visit campuses and meet with coaches.
- Send updated game DVDs to coaches.
- Ask advocates to call and write coaches on your behalf.
- Continue to review and edit your list of colleges.
- Continue preparing for standardized tests: Review the tests' schedule and sign up to take test(s). These tests are only offered on certain dates throughout the year.
- Decide which teachers you'd like to write a letter of recommendation for you and ask them if they would.

During the second half of the junior year and the first half of the senior year, the process of applying to colleges and recruiting yourself goes fast. Many student athletes might feel a bit overwhelmed with responsibilities, such as college visits, constant communication with coaches and other advisors both in high school and at the colleges, and hammering out the final list of college preferences. Student athletes also have to take stock of where they are in the recruiting process, and how they currently match up with their desired college choices. Don't be afraid to ask college coaches where you stand. This summer you should do the following:

- Start on your Common Application. Write required essay(s).
- Visit campuses and meet with coaches.
- Play on a travel or club team.
- Be in close contact with all relevant college coaches.
- Take standard tests: Gauge whether or not more attention is needed.
- Continue to develop your body, speed, agility and strength to prepare for collegiate level sports.
- Take on an internship, job or volunteer job.

The first semester of senior year will be insanely busy with schoolwork, applying to colleges, meeting with guidance counselors, and training for your last year of high school athletics. It can be a little overwhelming because of all that you need to juggle: school projects, college applications, and meetings with your college counselor, among other activities. It can be a very stressful time, but to put yourself in the best possible position to be recruited, the following need to be your top priorities:

- All grades and tests scores must be in order.
- You must be in close contact with all the relevant college coaches.
- Complete your Common Application.
- Get letters of recommendation from your teachers/guidance counselor.
- Complete your NCAA eligibility application.
- If possible, invite coaches to come see you play.
- After gaining admission to college(s), decide which one to attend.
- If you have no offers coming in, then ask coaches you've been in contact with if they have any colleagues who coach a program that you may be a better fit for. It is possible that your original list consists of colleges that are athletically or academically too high a level for you to succeed at, so you may want to consider some at a lower level or smaller size.

Chapter 12

# STREAMLINING THE PROCESS AS AN UPPERCLASSMAN

## Get the Ball Rolling

If you want to start recruiting yourself during your junior year—or even the beginning of your senior year—it's not too late. The window is smaller, but it's not closed. Get the ball rolling as quickly as possible:

1. Decide on your 10 "reach" schools, 10 "target" schools and 10 "safety" schools.
2. Email the coaches right away with your transcript and your player profile (see Chapter 16: Plays). You should include as much information as you can reasonably put into one email. Also send them a game DVD or a link to game highlights on YouTube or Vimeo.
3. Wait one week. If you don't hear anything back, place a follow-up phone call to the recruiting coordinator/coach.

If you don't hear back from anyone, you may continue to send information on yourself, and to call the coaches, but use your best judgment in deciding whether or not to pour time into an unresponsive school. This is why it's best to keep all of your options open, as long as possible.

Whatever you do, don't take any non-responsiveness on the part of a coach personally! Every college coach has unique needs, and you can never be sure what those needs are, or how they change; they are not a reflection of your talent as a student athlete. Anyway, you can only choose one college in the end.

Remember, if you do hear back from a coach, and the college seems interested in you, consider going for a visit or inviting one of the coaches to come see you play—on your high school team, if you're still in season, or on your club or travel team, if possible.

IMPORTANT: Keep adjusting and revising your list of colleges according to the level of interest you receive from each. Use your best judgment in intensifying your communication with the colleges that are interested and backing off from those that are not.

## If You're a Senior Who's "Late to the Game"

By the end of the fall of your senior year, it's probably too late to recruit yourself effectively, because most college teams will be set on their recruits. But even at this late period, you never know. If you fit the particular needs of a certain coach and team, you might still be in a position to receive an admissions offer. (Be advised that these cases will be rare.)

If you want to pursue a college after the fall of your senior year, do the following immediately:

- Email the college coach your profile, transcript, game film and game schedule.
- Wait no more than 48 hours for feedback; if you don't hear back, call, and have your high school, club or travel team coach email and call on your behalf. Persistent follow-up is crucial here.
- Ask the coach if their recruiting class is full. If so, move on to the next college on your list.
- Ask the coach, "If I can get admitted on my own, would there be a spot on the team for me?"
- Consider taking a gap year or post-grad year, which buys you more time to recruit yourself. This can be beneficial and could increase your chances to go to a college you are really interested in. See Chapter 15: Rare Scenarios for more information on this option.

## Chapter 13
# RESOURCE CENTER

The Your Recruiting Playbook Resource Center is designed to help provide you with additional information & sources to become better informed about the recruiting process. Remember, ultimately it's up to the student athlete to get recruited by colleges, do not wait for colleges to contact you. By being more knowledgeable and proactive with recruiting yourself, more opportunities and possibilities will be created. The resources below are purely meant to assist in YOU gaining knowledge. Your Recruiting Playbook does not receive any compensation nor endorse anyone particular of the resources below. Listed information & links are provided to help you become more educated on the recruiting process.

### NCAA, NAIA & NJCAA Official Websites:

National Collegiate Athletic Association
PO Box 6222, Indianapolis, IN 46206 • 888-388-9748 • **ncaa.org**

National Association of Intercollegiate Athletics
1200 Grand Boulevard, Kansas City, MO 64106 • 816-595-8000 • **naia.org**

National Junior College Athletic Association
1755 Telstar Drive, #103, Colorado Springs, CO • 719-590-9788 • **njcaa.org**

### Planning Tools to Shape Your Future

College Admissions: **inlikeme.com**
Big Future: **bigfuture.collegeboard.org**
Find Best College Fit For You: **colleges.niche.com**
US News: **usnews.com**
The Sallie Mae Fund: **thesalliemaefund.org**
NCAA Student: **http://web3.ncaa.org/ECWR2/NCAA_EMS/NCAA.jsp**
Campus Advisors: **campusadvisors.com**

## Getting the Cost of College Funded

10 Best Sites To Search for Scholarships: **colleges.usatoday.com**
Free Application for Federal Student Aid: **https://fafsa.gov/**
FinAid - Student Guide to Financial Aid: **fina id.org**
Free Education Guide: **freeeducationguide.com**
Financial planning for college: **studentloannetwork.com**

College Coaches Online is an affordable tool to assist student athletes with finding current contact information for all NCAA, NAIA and Junior College athletic programs. Find coaches names, addresses, emails and phone numbers in seconds. Search for colleges by specific needs: location, size, academics, tuition costs, sport and division: you personalize the list! **collegecoachesonline.com**

*"We want contact from the athletes. We want the athlete to be proactive, to take the initiative. If they can't pick up the phone to call or it's too much to return an email, I don't know that they're going to have that work ethic that we desire out of a student athlete. You can never bug a college coach too much. Unless they told you that they don't have a spot for you in their program. The more initiative you take, the more you show your desire to be in their program, the better. I'm looking for something that sets an athlete apart."*- Jennifer Mills, Head Coach, Women's Volleyball, Clarion University

*"Attended a live event by Steven Binder. My parents & I thought we knew the ins & outs of the recruiting process but, clearly, did not. His presentation had helpful information and gave us an action plan. His book was so easy to read and it taught us how to interact with college coaches. Thanks Steven, I recommend it to everyone who wants to play college sports."*- William, Soccer Player

*"We tried expensive recruiting services, recruiting counselors & coaches… they did not work & were expensive. Realized after reading Steven's book & calling him on the phone, we knew exactly what to do and how best to proceed. He is a true expert on college sports recruiting & better yet, he cares about helping people in a nurturing way."*
- Jose & Lucy C., Parents of a collegiate lacrosse player

Chapter 14

# RECRUITING AND VIDEO SERVICES

*When a young man writes a wellwritten, thoughtful email—that's clearly not something he cut and pasted my name and Bowdoin in—that really means something to us. We want to recruit kids that have done their research and feel that Bowdoin is a great place for them. We'll want to follow up with them and make sure to see them play, because they have genuine interest in us. The player that contacts us with a form email that he could have sent to thirty other coaches—we still follow up, but we're less inclined to be as excited about their interest in Bowdoin, given that we're not sure how sincere their interest is in our program. People often ask me about recruiting services—they certainly can be helpful, but I don't think they're a necessity in the recruiting process. You're probably better off spending your time and money on your academic qualifications.*
—Jason Archbell, Head Coach, Men's Lacrosse, Bowdoin College

In the course of playing high school sports and considering playing sports in college, you will come across recruiting and video services. I would neither outright endorse nor recommend against using these services—it's a personal decision for you. But I'd be remiss not to mention them in a guide to college athletics recruiting, not least because many of your fellow student athletes and their families will use or at least consider using them.

Using this playbook and using recruiting and video services are not mutually exclusive. You can certainly do both. However, I would advise anyone considering using one of these services to reflect on what they're getting for their money:
  • Filming of your games (adding graphics and other ornamentation to the film, e.g., highlighting/circling you on the field/court)

- Emailing/calling college coaches
- Finding/suggesting colleges for you.

None of these is something that you can't accomplish yourself, with the possible exception of adding graphics to your film. Even that is of uncertain value, as college coaches prefer simple, straightforward film that shows only whether or not a student athlete can *play*.

The biggest drawback to using these services is that in order to recruit yourself effectively, you must develop personal relationships with college coaches and earn their trust. If a recruiting service is communicating with coaches on behalf of hundreds, if not thousands, of other student athletes in addition to you, how personal can those communications really be? How deep can those relationships become if you're not cultivating them yourself? How can you earn trust without a personal relationship?

Additionally, while a recruiting service might be able to reach out to hundreds of colleges for you, or to recommend to you hundreds of schools, you'll ultimately be applying to approximately a dozen schools at most. You have to decide how much extra value these services offer. They are likely to provide you with lists of schools in which you may not be seriously interested.

Recruiting and video services can be helpful, but they can also be quite costly. Make sure you know what kind of "added value" you are getting before you enlist their services.

## Chapter 15
# RARE SCENARIOS

### Fifth-Year Prep Schools

In rare cases, a student athlete might consider playing an additional year of high school sports, post-graduation, by enrolling in a fifth-year prep school. Although this is uncommon, no playbook to college sports recruiting would be complete without addressing it.

A fifth-year prep school should only be considered if the student athlete, after graduating high school, is still relatively unprepared for college in two areas: physically and academically. Generally speaking, improving in one or both of these areas can help a student athlete either attain a more substantial scholarship (for instance, Division I or II, instead of III) or gain admission to a more "exclusive" school (for instance, a "reach" school rather than a "target" school).

However, attending a fifth-year prep school is not a mainstream decision. And it's an expensive decision: all fifth-year prep schools are private and require a year's tuition, and will most likely have boarding expenses. Therefore, a student athlete should only consider a fifth-year prep school if he or she is fairly positive it will make a difference in their college admission and life.

As always, you can gauge this by speaking directly to college coaches. If you feel you are a borderline recruit for a certain school, ask the coach: "Attending your college is my ultimate goal. Would attending a fifth-year prep school help me gain admission? Which one would you recommend?" College coaches will be straightforward in answering this question. Some coaches might actually recommend a particular prep school, if they have a relationship with it, or they may have alternative ideas for you.

The good news here is that you can apply to fifth-year prep schools and colleges simultaneously. In other words, you can wait to see which colleges you get into while applying to fifth-year prep schools and decide which course to take after you hear from every college.

---

**Time-out**

Due to the reputation of some fifth-year prep schools, there is a tendency to think that this is only an option for "jocks" who don't have many college options outside of sports. This is not so. I personally know a student athlete who gained admission to Haverford College (an academically prestigious school) with the help of a fifth year at a prep school.

---

BOTTOM LINE: If you're physically or psychologically young, a fifth-year prep school might be something to consider. However, you must be certain that this option will make a significant difference for you.

## If You Get Hurt

Another rare scenario that is important to cover is the misfortune of a student athlete sustaining an injury that keeps him or her off the court or field for an extended period of time.

IMPORTANT: If you get hurt, immediately call or email all the coaches you're in contact with and let them know what happened.

The good news is that college coaches are used to this happening occasionally. It should not affect your recruiting prospects at all, as long as you can ultimately get back on the field of play and show any prospective college coaches that you are healed.

In fact, your time on the sidelines is a good opportunity to intensify your contact with coaches and *to really prove your character* to them. You can do this in your emails and other communications by doing the following:

- Keep them up-to-date on your grades.
- Keep them up-to-date on the progress of your rehab.
- Send them short training clips (for example: "Hey Coach – Please check this out. My ankle is feeling much better and my movement is back!").
- Show the coaches that you're not only passionate as an athlete, you're a passionate person:
  - Get involved in a community service project you otherwise would not have time for.
  - Become a de-facto assistant coach on your high school or travel team, and tell the college coaches all about it.
- Generally speaking, show the college coaches that you can persevere without playing. They need to know that. Should you get injured while playing for them or otherwise not get much playing time in college, you'll remain a team player, a valuable asset to their squad.

---

**Time-out**

I know it's not easy sitting out; I've been there myself. But getting injured provides even more incentive to recruit yourself in the manner I've discussed throughout this playbook. It's a time to make your relationships with college coaches even stronger!

---

NOTE: If you've already signed a letter of intent, the admissions offer cannot be rescinded. But you'd still be wise to keep your college coach up-to-date on your progress.

**Chapter 16**

# PLAYS: GET RECRUITED

*Some elite athletes, we find them. But everyone else we recruit, they contact us.*
—Andy Ma, Head Coach, Fencing, University of Pennsylvania

**N**ow that you've read *Your Recruiting Playbook,* here are the plays! In this chapter, you will find the samples of the plays you need to execute to recruit yourself:

1. **Student Athlete Personal Profile**

   a. This is your athletic and academic resume. You should have an updated version with you at all times—especially whenever you're competing in a tournament, showcase, or visiting a college. You never know which coaches are going to show up!

   b. Whenever you make an update to your profile, be sure to email the new version to the coaches you're in contact with. It's yet another opportunity for communication.

2. **Introductory Email**

   (suggested topics for writing to coaches; see Chapter 9)

3. **During and End-of-Season Emails**

4. **Student Athlete's College Coaches Contact List**

5. **Pros and Cons List** (to note thoughts after college visits)

6. **Important Actions Checklist**

   (to help make sure you're on the right path)

---

**Time-out**

Don't forget to download the *NCAA Guide for the College-Bound Student Athlete.* You need to know the rules that affect you—especially since they change quite often:
**ncaapublications.com**

---

## SAMPLE I: Student Athlete Personal Profile*

NOTE: Use this template to record your personal information and athletic accomplishments. This is your personal athletic resume.

**Your Name**
Address
City, State, Zip-Code
Telephone
Email: youremail@gmail.com
Social Media Handles and Addresses

Action Photo Here

Height and weight
Position: 3 and 4—agile defender, strong rebounder,
    solid low-post passer

**Objective**
To be a key contributor on a college basketball team while receiving an excellent education.

**Education**
- Your High School: Street, City, State, Zip Code; Junior, Class of 2016; Guidance Counselor's Name and Telephone
- GPA 3.2 with three advanced courses. SATs or ACTs: (list actual test scores)
- Academic or school achievements: (honor roll, class rank, accomplished musician or artist, etc.)

**High School Stats**
- Through 3 years of high school: XXX points, XXX rebounds or XXX assists
- Led team in 3-point shooting and rebounding
- As a junior, starter and key contributor to Your High School's 2014/2015 league playoffs
- 2nd on team in the following: Scoring: XX ppg, Assists X.X apg and Rebounds X.X rpg
- Led team in free throws, 81%.
- Team Captain

*Profile should be on one page, but if your accolades and awards warrant a second page, go for it.*

## Team Achievements
- Connecticut High School Quarter Finalist, 2014
- Finished tied for second in CT Conference, 2015

## Individual High School Achievement Awards
- Wendy's High School Heisman Nominee, 2014
- All-Conference Honorable Mention Team
- Metro Athletic Association All-Star 2015 Classic Selection
- Blank HS Holiday Tournament – MVP, 2014
- Blank HS Holiday All-Tournament Team – 2015

## Outside Achievements and Awards
- US Nationals Championship All-Star Team, Texas, AAU Tournament, 2015

## AAU/Travel Team, High School Coach, Trainer
- AAU Coach's Name, Name of Team, Telephone
- High School Coach's Name, High School, Head Coach, Telephone
- Trainer's Name: Company, Professional Skills Trainer, Telephone

## Personal Interests
- Community service: volunteer at Habitat for Humanity
- Working with children at disabilities camps, travel, reading
- Studying to become bilingual in French
- Ceramics

## Highlights and Full Game DVDs Available

## SAMPLE II: Student Athlete Personal Profile*

**Your Name**
Street
City, State, Zip Code
Telephone
E-mail: youremail@gmail.com
Social Media Handles and Addresses

Action Photo Here

Height and Weight
Position: Midfielder: agile defender, aggressive scorer.

**Objective**
To be a key contributor on a college soccer team while receiving an excellent education.

**Education**
- Name of High School, School Address, City, State, Zip Code; Junior, Class of 2016; Counselor's name, Guidance Counselor Telephone
- GPA 2.7 with one advanced course. SATs or ACTs (list actual test scores)
- Academic or school achievements: (honor roll, class rank, accomplished musician or artist, etc.)

*Profile should be on one page, but if your accolades and awards warrant a second page, go for it.*

## Personal Awards/Team Accomplishments
- Through 3 years of high school: XX goals, XX assists
- Led team in penalty shot goals scored
- As a junior, this past season, key starter and contributor to Your High School's 2014/2015 League Elite Eight
- 3rd on team in the following: Scoring: X.X gpg, Assists X.X pg
- Led team in minutes played
- All-District Honorable Mention
- All-Conference Honorable Mention

## High School Coach
Coach's Name, Telephone, Email: coachemail@gmail.com

## Travel Team: Premier 16s
Coach's Name, Telephone, Email: coachname@aol.com

## Skills/Conditioning Trainer
Trainer's name, Telephone

## Personal Interests
- Community service: volunteer at Power Laces for Kids
- Working with children at Education for Athletes Camps, travel, reading
- Enjoy music and playing the piano

## Highlights and Full Game DVDs Available

## SAMPLE: Introductory Email

*Note: Highlight your personal athletic accomplishments in the body of this email.*

Your Name
Telephone
youremail@aol.com
Social Media Handles & Addresses

Date

Dear Coach *Name*:

I would like to introduce myself. My name is _____ and I am very interested in attending _____ as a student athlete. Enclosed please find my profile, AAU schedule, a press clipping and game film.

A few highlights are:
- My high school team plays a highly competitive schedule and up-tempo style.
- I was 2nd on the team in scoring, rebounds, assists and steals.
- Selected to the Section Eleven All-League team
- *(Can list non-athletic highlights if you choose)*

*(Finally, add in a line that is specific to the school you are writing to. Something of interest to you, that shows that you have done your homework on and reflects your genuine interest in the school.)*

Looking forward to speaking to you soon.

Sincerely,

Your Name

## Topics That Will Help You Stay in Constant Communication with College Coaches

*Writing frequent, personal, knowledgeable notes to college coaches is crucial!*

As mentioned earlier, here are some suggested topics for emails/handwritten notes to coaches, which can cover many subjects, including:

- How school is going for you
- A big upcoming game
- Your team's schedule
- Awards
- Current events (shows you have other interests)
- A big win
- An academic achievement
- An athletic achievement
- If you're selected as captain of your team (shows leadership)
- Game DVD
- Your community service
- How your team is doing
- High school schedule
- Camps/clinics you're attending
- A desire to come to campus
  - "I'm coming to campus in a few weeks, will you be around?" or "I might be at the School A versus School B game, will you be there?" After a visit, send the coach an email, even if you didn't see him.

Remember that coaches like it when student athletes write to them about their own programs. Here are some suggested topics you can write about:

- When an assistant coach is hired
- A big upcoming game
- A noteworthy event regarding that college (find news about the school on the internet)
- The college coach—or the program—reaches a milestone
- A big win
- A rivalry game

## SAMPLE: During and End-of-Season Emails

Emails should be written during and at the end of each high school and travel/club team season.

**Time-out**

You should develop several types of notes like this. College coaches want to hear from you—the more the better. Each communication should reflect your "personal touch."

Your Name
Telephone
youremail@aol.com

Hello again Coach *Name:*

Congratulations on your season! I'm sure you would have liked to win your conference championship, but it must be gratifying to have won ten more games than last season.

My high school team had a similar season. We fell short in our conference tournament, but we made it to the second round for the first time since 2006!

Personally, I was happy to meet some of my main goals for the season:
- Averaged X points (or goals) per game—
  2 more than last year
- Led my division in assists per game
- Was again selected to the Section Eleven
  All-League team
- Got a B+ in organic chemistry—that might be the
  highlight of highlights!

I'm very much looking forward to speaking with you again soon.

Best wishes,
Your Name

P.S. I have attached my updated profile.

## College Coaches Contact List

The spreadsheet below is used to organize all the pertinent information you will need to recruit yourself to college coaches. All this information can be found on a college's website.

**COLLEGE**

COACH

ADDRESS

EMAIL                                         PHONE

**COLLEGE**

COACH

ADDRESS

EMAIL                                         PHONE

**COLLEGE**

COACH

ADDRESS

EMAIL                                         PHONE

**COLLEGE**

COACH

ADDRESS

EMAIL                                         PHONE

**COLLEGE**

COACH

ADDRESS

EMAIL                                         PHONE

**COLLEGE**

COACH

ADDRESS

EMAIL                                         PHONE

**COLLEGE**

COACH

ADDRESS

EMAIL PHONE

**COLLEGE**

COACH

ADDRESS

EMAIL PHONE

**COLLEGE**

COACH

ADDRESS

EMAIL PHONE

**COLLEGE**

COACH

ADDRESS

EMAIL PHONE

**COLLEGE**

COACH

ADDRESS

EMAIL PHONE

**COLLEGE**

COACH

ADDRESS

EMAIL PHONE

**COLLEGE**

COACH

ADDRESS

EMAIL PHONE

This is a valuable list to compile because as time passes, it might not be easy to remember the smaller but crucial differences between colleges.

Writing down what you like/dislike will also help you think about it all in a more objective way. Take pictures as a way of remembering finer points of a college. It can be difficult to remember specifics when you are visiting a number of schools. To help shape your impressions when visiting a college, here are some things to consider: talk to students while you are on campus, sit in on a class that might interest you, eat in the cafeteria. Other considerations include the location of school, how far from home you wish to travel, or your preference for a particular climate.

**College:** _____

(List anything that's important to you: location, beauty of campus, students, alumni networking, academics, food, coach, team, gym, social life, etc.)

| PROS | CONS |
| --- | --- |
| | |

## Important Actions Checklist

*Are you doing the following?*

1. Continually develop your list of 10 "reach" schools, 10 "target" schools and 10 "safety" schools.
2. Make sure you are on track in completing the core classes needed for NCAA eligibility.
3. Make sure you are taking the necessary standardized tests. *And don't forget to report test scores to the NCAA Eligibility Center.*
4. Consistently email and call college coaches to develop relationships with them.
5. Consistently update your student athlete profile and send out DVDs (or YouTube/Vimeo links).
6. Work on improving your skills and fundamentals.
7. Branch out and gain exposure to as many college coaches as possible. And attend showcases.
8. Visit colleges to get a feel of what you like and don't like.
9. Get feedback from college coaches on your athletic ability and academic performance.
10. Get your support team involved: high school and/or travel coaches, guidance counselors, anyone who can advocate for you.
11. Review college team websites to gauge their rosters—do they need your position or a player like you?
12. Speak to the alumni or current/former players of colleges you're interested in—the more knowledge you have, the better!
13. Be courteous and respectful, and follow up with college coaches.

---

### Time-out for Parents

This checklist is an important area you can help your student athlete manage. Your support is crucial in helping them stay committed to the process throughout their high school years.

---

## Chapter 17
# SOME FINAL THOUGHTS

*If I did not reach out to college coaches myself, I would not have played. It definitely gave me the edge. Then, playing sports in college allowed me to build relationships with alumni who are passionate about helping student athletes.*
—Andrea, hockey player, Michigan

Once you've accepted an admission offer, you're pretty much all set. You should be proud of yourself on a job well done. And if I don't begrudge you a little "senioritis," I hope you won't begrudge me a few additional words of wisdom on the years ahead.

Athletics have helped you get into college and will obviously be a significant part of your college experience. But bear in mind that college is just as much about your academic and social growth. Make sure to develop yourself in those areas with the same vivacity and sense of character with which you have nurtured your athletic gifts.

*These next four years will fly by. Make sure you squeeze the most out of them.*

Here are some final thoughts:
- Keep in mind that everybody who comes to your college team was a premier, elite player in his or her region also.
  - So over the spring, summer and fall, it's very important to keep working. It's difficult to make a second first impression.
- Continue to talk to your future coach:
  - "What's your conditioning program? I want to be part of your playing rotation. That's my goal. I'm willing to work for it." (There's nothing wrong with saying that. Having a plan is a smart thing.)

Summer-before-freshman-year checklist:
- Conditioning plan:
  - Improve speed and quickness
  - Weight training
  - Work on specific skills
  - Reach out to returning players, build relationships, ask questions
  - Don't let up now—*keep up the momentum*
- Remember what brought you here—hard work plus talent

At college, network with alumni, professors and coaches. These relationships can last a lifetime. Plus, they can lead to internships and employment.

**GOOD LUCK!**

# Chapter 18
# TESTIMONIALS ON RECRUITING YOURSELF

## College Coaches

*The recruiting process is a difficult and long path to success. The more knowledge and understanding about the recruiting process you have, the better chance you have playing at any level in college.*
—Geno Auriemma, Women's Basketball, University of Connecticut

*The more we hear from a recruit, the higher their chances are to make the team. It's like the saying "the squeaky wheel get's the oil." If a recruit is persistent with us, it shows they have a strong desire to be a part of our program and those are the types of kids you want. If you have a spot on the team and you are deciding who to give it to, it will probably be the visible, persistent recruit.*
—Corrie Falcon, Head Coach, Swimming and Diving, UC San Diego

*When I first started thirteen years ago, a lot of recruiting was done by going to see a student athlete play, by word of mouth, or referrals. Now the majority of the initial contact is through recruiting services or through student athletes themselves.*
—Matt Magers, Head Coach, Baseball, Minnesota State University

*Some elite athletes—we find them. But everyone else we recruit—they contact us.*
—Andy Ma, Head Coach, Fencing, University of Pennsylvania

*Owning the recruiting process is the smartest thing you can do regardless whether you are a Division I, II or III caliber athlete in any sport. Being proactive with college coaches about your interest, profile, ability and academics can help you with getting recruited. Also, staying engaged*

about the college team helps a student athlete show they are sincerely interested in that school. Coaches can tell when people have and have not done their preparation. Be your own best advocate and stay informed.
—Lindsay Gottlieb, Head Coach, Women's Basketball,
  University of California, Berkeley

Every year, we start with 15,000 to 20,000 student athletes nationwide who fit our profile for football. On any given day, I get between 10 and 15 emails from prospects. If they're from my area, I try to watch their video immediately, and to look at their profile. The more information and contact with the coaches, the better. You can never get too much information out there about yourself. All things being equal—academics, skill set, position—if we know a recruit is extremely interested in Dartmouth, then that would definitely increase his stock.
— Christopher Wilkerson, Head Coach Football Coach, University of
  Chicago (formerly Recruiting Coordinator, Dartmouth College)

We want contact from the athletes. We want the athlete to be proactive, to take the initiative. If they can't pick up the phone to call or it's too much to return an email, I don't know that they're going to have that work ethic that we desire out of a student athlete. You can never bug a college coach too much. Unless they told you that they don't have a spot for you in their program. The more initiative you take, the more you show your desire to be in their program, the better. I'm looking for something that sets an athlete apart.
—Jennifer Mills, Head Coach, Women's Volleyball, Clarion University

It's very important to get your name out there with coaches. Email is a great way to communicate. In your junior or sophomore year, it's important to have contact with coaching staffs. We like to see enthusiastic student athletes. We love to coach student athletes who really want to be a part of our college and campus community.
—Jeff Brown, Head Coach, Basketball, Middlebury College

*When a young man writes a wellwritten, thoughtful email—that's clearly not something he cut and pasted my name and Bowdoin in—that really means something to us. We want to recruit kids that have done their research and feel that Bowdoin is a great place for them. We'll want to follow up with them and make sure to see them play, because they have genuine interest in us. The player that contacts us with a form email that he could have sent to thirty other coaches—we still follow up, but we're less inclined to be as excited about their interest in Bowdoin, given that we're not sure how sincere their interest is in our program. People often ask me about recruiting services—they certainly can be helpful, but I don't think they're a necessity in the recruiting process. You're probably better off spending your time and money on your academic qualifications.*
—Jason Archbell, Head Coach, Men's Lacrosse, Bowdoin College

*I much prefer getting an email or phone call directly from a prospect or his coach as opposed from a recruiting service that just sends blanket emails to every school in the country. I want to know, A: That they are interested in our institution, and, B: Why they are interested in our institution. I want them to let me know in that first brief introductory email that they have researched our institution and that they know something about it and that they know it is a possible fit academically, socially, and geographically, etc.*
—Trevor Andrews, Recruiting Coordinator and Defensive Line Coach, Football, College of William and Mary

*If we're looking at two players with the same ability, and we can't take them both, obviously the one who shows more interest, who comes to visit first, is going to be higher on our list. Being proactive is absolutely going to help. Every level is different... When I was at a smaller division one school, we would go watch most student athletes who wrote to us, especially the ones who played in a specific position that was needed at that time.*
—Tatum Clowney, Assistant Coach, Women's Soccer, University of Alabama

## Parents, High School/Travel Coaches, Sportswriters, Professionals

*Steven Binder has been a blessing to our program at Mount Vernon High School. At the Binderhoops Basketball Showcases, he is superb in his presentation to the student-athletes. He lays out their priorities in a manner that is both easily understood and attainable. Steven is able to "Cut through" all of the bad information out there and give each and every youngster a blueprint of what their course towards success should be. This is not only helpful to the "star athlete" but really beneficial to ALL of our players.*

*At our Mount Vernon Summer Camp, Mr. Binder has again given of himself to help our student-athletes gain a better focus of the big picture. He does not ruin dreams, but he brings a focus on reality engaging our youngsters in a fashion to "Attack their goals." Steven has a gift for delivering his "Pitch for success" with basketball, a little comic relief, and real life experiences all encompassed into one package.*
—Robert Cimmino, Athletic Director and Head Boy's Varsity
   Basketball Coach, Mount Vernon High School, NY

*The recruiting process is long and arduous; it's emotional and stressful. Its very important that the family band together and get started early with a plan.*
—Susan, parent of a high school student athlete, New York

*This is the most sensible, useful guide for high school athletes that I've ever read. I just wish I'd read Steve Binder's book before I sent four athletes off to college.*
—Steve Wulf, sports journalist, author and parent of student athletes

*So many good players and only a few spots ... we needed a smart way to get noticed by college coaches and scouts, recruiting yourself was the difference maker for one of my players to be selected over someone else.*
—Manny, regional travel team coach, Illinois

*We had no idea about college recruiting, spent money on recruiting services and read lots of information on the internet and none of it helped us take action that worked. His approach of understanding the college recruiting process and the simple action steps to take allowed our child the opportunity to play college athletics. Steven's information is the difference maker.*
—Karen and John, parents of a college student athlete, New York

*Steven Binder grounds the parents and players in critical thinking and planning that can really assist you at any age. He stresses how recruiting yourself and building relationships with college coaches is key. His plan allows you to take immediate action.*
—Henry, parent of a high school athlete, Pennsylvania

*College sports changed the life of my child. It only happened because we reached out to college coaches first. Steven Binder has over 25 years of experience in helping players get recruited. His simple plan works.*
—Arlene, parent of high school and college athlete, North Carolina.

*There are so many kids who play high school sports. There isn't much difference between many of them. So recruiting yourself goes a long way. It shows you're serious. The college coach thinks, "This is a kid I can work with. The other kid, I'm not sure—I'd have to make ten phone calls, five emails." Out of the 50 or so student athletes I've coached who have played in college, at least 30 of them were advised by Steven Binder.*
—Pat Mangan, Head Coach, Boys Basketball,
    Frederick Douglass Academy

*The student-athlete experience in college can be rich, vast and rewarding for a young adult. For both students and parents, there are important steps to be taken in the process. For those who have the mission of participating in college athletics, Steven Binder provides an honest and insightful road map on how to achieve that goal.*
—Sunil Gulati, President, U.S. Soccer Federation

*The access to college sports for aspiring student athletes is daunting. At long last, "Your Recruiting Playbook," with its guidance and advice, helps you navigate the process. Well done!*

—Donna Orender, Owner of Orender Unlimited, Former Top Executive of the PGA TOUR and WNBA, parent of student athletes

*YOUR RECRUITING PLAYBOOK is a simple, step-by-step guide of how to get recruited for college sports. It can help you play any sport at the NCAA Division I, II or III level. The information and take-action content of the book will allow you to be insightful about the recruiting process.*

—Marcellus Wiley, Ivy League Hall of Fame, Former NFL All-Pro Player, ESPN Host of SportsNation and Max & Marcellus

## Student Athletes

*Recruiting yourself is so important. It improved my chances with many more colleges. Steven Binder's step-by-step process is simple to follow and put into action.*

—Michael, football player, Georgia

*There are so many good players out there, I needed to stand out. Recruiting yourself works and helps build relationships with college coaches.*

—Sarah, soccer and lacrosse player, California

*If I did not reach out to college coaches myself, I would not have played. It definitely gave me the edge. Then, playing sports in college allowed me to build relationships with alumni who are passionate about helping student athletes.*

—Andrea, hockey player, Michigan

*Once I became a recruited athlete, the process allowed me more choices and I went to a better college than I thought was possible.*

—Brendan, baseball player, Florida

*I needed help. I did not know what to do. The internet has a lot of information, but it's not easy to understand. Recruiting yourself and proving yourself to college coaches allowed me to create opportunities. Thanks to Binder's process, my coach, my parents and I now understand what to do and how to take action.*
—John, football player, Texas

*Recruiting yourself works. I had average talent and grades. By consistently communicating with college coaches, a trust was built, and I earned a spot.*
—Jennifer, basketball player, Rhode Island

*I was not being recruited at all before I used the simple step-by-step action plan outlined in YOUR RECRUITING PLAYBOOK. After recruiting myself to college coaches, I received 6 offers.*
—Kevin, basketball player, New York

# Your Own Plays, Thoughts & Reminders

# Your Own Plays, Thoughts & Reminders